D1527314

MISFORTUNE ON CLEVELAND'S
Millionaires' Row

MISFORTUNE ON CLEVELAND'S
Millionaires' Row

ALAN F. DUTKA

THE
History
PRESS

Published by The History Press
Charleston, SC 29403
www.historypress.net

Copyright © 2015 by Alan F. Dutka
All rights reserved

First published 2015

ISBN 978.1.54020.239.0

Library of Congress Control Number: 2015936859

Contents

Contents

Preface

B ack in 1937, Ella Grant Wilson completed the second of her two
books documenting the homes and families of Euclid Avenue during
the street's most prestigious period. As a florist catering to the wealthy,
Wilson had access to many, if not most, of the residences and their owners;
millionaire Charles Brush even invested in her floral business. Through her
knowledge and anecdotes, Wilson demonstrated a total grasp of Euclid
Avenue's historical importance.

A decade after the publication of the book, I made my first visit to a Euclid
Avenue mansion. As a five-year-old boy, I really didn't appreciate or care
about the architecture and history of Leonard Hanna's stunning home. My
immediate interest concerned a much older historical period when dinosaurs
roamed the earth. Much to my amusement, their bones sat on display in the
old mansion, then the home of the Cleveland Museum of Natural History.
Thirteen years afterward, I initiated the first in a series of annual visits to
the Samuel Mather mansion, located just west of where the Hanna home,
now a victim of the Innerbelt Freeway, had stood. Gaining maturity, the
grandeur of Mather's home did impress me as I patiently waited in line to
obtain license plates at the American Automobile Association, the mansion's
owner at the time.

As an adult, I discovered a wealth of information about Cleveland's
magnificent Millionaires' Row. George E. Condon devoted a chapter to
Euclid Avenue in each of his classic books, *Cleveland: The Best Kept Secret* (1967)
and *Cleveland: Prodigy of the Western Reserve* (1979). Cleveland newspapers

published many nostalgic articles reminiscing about the city's millionaires and their luxurious homes; scholarly journals also paid homage to the past glory of Euclid Avenue. Students throughout the country conducted research and authored PhD dissertations about the fabled street.

In 1991, the Western Reserve Historical Society launched a landmark exhibition about Millionaires' Row. In conjunction with the show, Kent State University published *Showplace of America*, Jan Cigliano's masterful companion volume. Five years later, the Cleveland Convention Center's FloralScape (flower show) re-created portions of the homes' elegant gardens. In 2002, Richard E. Karberg and James A. Toman contributed the popular book *Euclid Avenue: Cleveland's Sophisticated Lady*. The Western Reserve Historical Society soon staged another exhibition, this time concentrating on "The Legacy of Euclid Avenue." Co-writing with Dan Ruminski, I authored material about the legendary street in the recently published *Cleveland in the Gilded Age*.

With the attention already given to Millionaires' Row, a valid question arises as to why yet another volume about the celebrated street is necessary. The vast majority of past material has emphasized the extravagant homes, formal social lives or business careers of Euclid Avenue residents. Yet very little has been written regarding other aspects of life on Millionaires' Row. Some of Euclid Avenue's residents participated in reprehensible scandals, experienced horrifying tragedies and fashioned shady business practices. This book presents stories that help fill these previously unexplored parts of life on what once composed the wealthiest street in the world.

In discussing street names and numbers, please note Clevelanders once referred to East Ninth Street as Erie Street, East Fifty-fifth Street as Willson Street and East Seventy-first Street as Giddings Avenue. Euclid Avenue's addresses have undergone two changes, one in 1906 and an earlier alteration in the 1880s. To circumvent tiresome cross-references, I have consistently used current street names and numbers throughout the book.

Acknowledgements

CLEVELAND PUBLIC LIBRARY
Margaret Baughman (Photographs)
Stacie Brisker (Special Collections)
Kelly Ross Brown (Fine Arts & Special Collections)
William Chase (Fine Arts & Special Collections)
Nicholas Durda (Photographs)
Thomas Edwards (History)
Pamela J. Eyerdam (Fine Arts & Special Collections)
Patrice Hamiter (Photographs)
Sabrina Laureano-Rosario (History)
Michael Jacobs (Special Collections)
Danilo Milich (History)
Ann Marie Wieland (Archives)
Chris Wood (History)

CLEVELAND STATE UNIVERSITY
William C. Barrow (Special Collections)
William Becker (Archives)
Lynn M. Duchez Bycko (Special Collections)

INDIVIDUALS
Deanna Dubiel
Priscilla Dutka
Diane D. Ghorbanzadeh
Mo Ghorbanzadeh
David Horan

THE HISTORY PRESS
Krista Slavicek
Hilary Parrish
Anna Burrous
Mustafa Walker
Mike Parsons
Danielle Raub

Introduction

C harles Lathrop Pack, one of America's wealthiest men, once recalled being lost in Germany's Black Forest. As evening approached, he discovered an isolated hut, his first view of civilization in hours. Desperately desiring shelter for the night, Pack engaged in a conversation with the hut's owner, who suspiciously peered down from a second-story window. The hut keeper, discovering Pack resided in Cleveland, asked if he lived on Euclid Avenue. When Pack responded in the affirmative, the owner promptly unbarred the door and invited Pack to stay the night. The fame of Euclid Avenue had penetrated even a secluded spot in the Black Forest.

Euclid Avenue's ascent to international prominence began about the time the Civil War ended. In 1866, the *Plain Dealer* observed, "Some of the private residences that are raising their grand heads on Euclid Avenue will cost sums that would cause a poor man's eyes to stare in amazement." In actuality, the mansions caused the poor, the rich and those in between all to stare in amazement.

The avenue acquired a deserved reputation as "Millionaires' Row" although the residences never approached the grandeur of George W. Vanderbilt's Biltmore in North Carolina or Cornelius Vanderbilt's Breakers in Rhode Island. In fact, even Euclid Avenue's millionaires constructed more impressive homes in other parts of the country, such as John D. Rockefeller's Kykuit in Pocantico Hills, New York, or Harry Flagler's Marble Casa in Palm Beach, Florida. Yet no street in the world except Euclid Avenue could

In the 1870s, the Euclid Avenue mansions of John Hay, Amasa Stone and Samuel L. Mather (all to the left) testified to the city's prosperity. *Courtesy of Cleveland Public Library, Photograph Collection.*

Five prominent Clevelanders constructed these consecutive Euclid Avenue mansions: Charles Bingham, Harry Devereux, Samuel Mather, Leonard Hanna and Charles Hickox. *Courtesy of Special Collections, Michael Schwartz Library, Cleveland State University.*

lay claim to so many impressive homes, built side by side, along a continuous stretch extending for about three miles.

Euclid Avenue residents engaged in quaint afternoon teas, formal dinners, extravagant evening parties, summer lawn concerts and holiday open houses. Their homes served as settings for debutante balls, wedding receptions, birthday and anniversary celebrations and somber funerals.

Residents of Euclid Avenue also encountered their share of far-from-idyllic incidents. The street's wealth stimulated criminal activity; robbers, muggers and burglars deemed the millionaires both lucrative and easy prey. One captured felon described his well-planned methodology to steal from the wealthy inhabitants. Obtaining a job as a grocery store delivery person, he intentionally cultivated friendly relationships with servants and coachmen employed by the millionaires; the workers unwittingly provided details such as the homeowners' evening plans. This insider information led to a string of very profitable burglaries.

In 1894, police arrested twenty-year-old Emma Moskewitz, a professional thief. Emma, employed as a domestic in wealthy homes, learned where her rich employers stored valuable but rarely used items such as china and silver tableware, silks, laces and expensive dresses. After stealing many of these items, she ended her employment before being discovered. Emma then moved on to her next victim using a new assumed name. Her arrest occurred after the family of Euclid Avenue millionaire George Worthington detected numerous valuable items missing from their home soon after she severed her employment.

Of a more violent nature, physical attacks took place on the lawns and even in the homes of millionaires. As early as 1867, a criminal assaulted and attempted to rape a female on the sidewalk in one of Euclid Avenue's most stylish sections.

Yet outsiders did not instigate all the unsavory behavior. Euclid Avenue residents created their own share of sensational scandals, engaged in distasteful business dealings, evaded the law and also endured incredible tragedies. Their enormous wealth could not prevent, and sometimes even contributed to, the failure and despair that, in extreme situations, led to jail sentences, suicide and murder. Sixteen examples of the traumas and anguish experienced by Euclid Avenue millionaires are presented in this book.

Part I
Affairs, Infidelity and Betrayal

Chapter 1

Multiple Affairs to Remember

The elopement of Nonnie May Stewart and George Ely Worthington deprived Euclid Avenue's society of what would certainly have been one of the most important social events of the year. But the couple's brief, scandal-ridden marriage provided spicy gossip for years to come.

Nonnie, born in 1878 to a wealthy Zanesville merchant, relocated to Cleveland as a child. Her father, William Charles Stewart, prospered as president of the Forest City Stone Company. The business mined sandstone in Euclid Township (now South Euclid) and sold stones used for window caps and sills, steps, landings, porches and sidewalks.

Born into wealth, Nonnie May Stewart acquired even more riches through marriage and then became a princess. *Courtesy of the* Cleveland Press.

Through hard work and excellent business sense, George Worthington turned a small amount of money into a national hardware empire. *Courtesy of Cleveland Public Library, Photograph Collection.*

By 1900, the Stewart family had joined Cleveland's upper crust by purchasing a Euclid Avenue home.

Nonnie attended elementary school on Carnegie Avenue near East Fifty-fifth Street; her classmates remembered her as bright, vivacious and high-spirited. Several of her peers predicted she would someday be a princess, but Nonnie scoffed at the idea, claiming she desired a wealthy, "real" man instead of a stuffy prince. Yet in her short forty-five-year life, Nonnie accomplished both by marrying into families of wealth and royalty.

As the son of Ralph Worthington and grandson of industrialist George Worthington, George Ely resided on or near Millionaires' Row from the time of his birth. His grandfather, at the age of seventeen, had acquired a job as a hardware store clerk in Cooperstown, New York. Four years later, he relocated to Cleveland with little money but enough ambition to establish his own hardware business. He traveled hundreds of miles on horseback throughout the country selling his products and establishing business relationships. His company expanded into a national wholesale operation, and he also founded the Cleveland Iron and Nail Company, invested in mining and blast furnace companies and served as president of the First National Bank of Cleveland.

Without the burdens of building a business from the ground up, Ralph successfully managed his father's hardware company while still allowing time for spirited and occasionally precarious hunting trips. On one of these outings, Ralph barely survived an unnerving attack by three Wyoming grizzly bears. The animals knocked him down, bit his leg and tore flesh from his body. Their assault ended prematurely when one bear bit into Ralph's coat, igniting a box of matches and scaring the assailants into retreat.

On October 1, 1894, George Ely and Nonnie eloped. At the age of twenty-two, George had not yet entered the Gilded Age business world, while eighteen-year-old Nonnie had just reached the legal marriage age. Reverend Arthur G. Upham, pastor of a Prospect Avenue Baptist church near East Forty-sixth Street, married the couple in his home, even though he had never met either one prior to the wedding. At the conclusion of the brief ceremony, George and Nonnie hurried to the old lakefront station, where they boarded a train headed for New York City.

Lewis Ford, the only member of the wedding party besides the bride, groom and minister, delivered letters to the couple's families announcing their already-in-progress elopement. Regarding the reactions of the parents, the *Cleveland Press* noted, "The youthfulness of the contracting parties was the only objection to the wedding" but then incorrectly speculated, "Doubtless all will be forgiven now."

The couple resided first on East Fifty-fifth Street and soon after on Sibley Street, at the time known as the "son-in-law street" because many newly married daughters of Euclid Avenue millionaires elected to reside on Sibley, a road between Euclid and Prospect Avenues near East Fifty-fifth Street. Youthful George rapidly ascended to secretary of his father-in-law's stone company. He commanded special respect as an expert pigeon shooter, a popular sport at the time, and soon developed a reputation for staying out late without the accompaniment of his wife. In quiet conversation, Euclid Avenue's society often chatted about the most recent reports of George and Nonnie's marriage tribulations and speculated about the timing of their anticipated separation.

The marriage did not survive five years; the uncontested divorce hearing required less than fifteen minutes to complete. Nonnie charged George with gross neglect and violation of his marriage vows. She testified her husband spent a great deal of his money on guns, ammunition and other women, although not always in that order. She depended completely on her father and grandparents for support, without which she would have been destitute. Nonnie didn't ask for alimony, and as her future unfolded, she certainly didn't need it. Not surprisingly, George lost his executive position at the stone company.

Following the divorce, George filed an alienation of affections lawsuit, demanding Frederick Mortimore Nicholas pay $50,000 in damages. According to George, he and Nonnie had lived happily and peacefully for about two years until Frederick entered his wife's life. As her lover, Frederick prejudiced and poisoned the mind of Nonnie by telling her she had made

Charismatic Frederick Mortimore Nicholas used an excellent singing voice and captivating charm to lure Nonnie May Stewart into an affair that ended both of their marriages. *Courtesy of the Cleveland Press.*

a mistake in marrying someone so substantially inferior to Frederick in every way. George claimed Nonnie and Frederick conferred as to "the best way of getting rid of me" and "carried on one continuous joyous love fest with each other." Frederick even intended to place his photograph in an expensive pair of buckle garters he had purchased for Nonnie, but the plan failed when George discovered the intimate Victorian garment. In a strangely modified *ménage a trois*, Nonnie, so enamored with Frederick, refused to attend the theater with George unless Frederick accompanied them.

The son of J.W. Nicholas, an extremely wealthy capitalist and vessel owner, Frederick exuded a great deal of charisma and sex appeal. In addition to coming from a rich family, he enjoyed singing. A splendid tenor voice made him very popular within musical circles and among church choirs. He further enhanced his celebrity status with memberships in the Hermit Club, Singers' Club and Shaker Country Club.

Frederick encountered his share of obstacles as he courted George's wife. On one occasion, in a very one-sided fistfight, George severely bloodied Frederick's face. As Nonnie and a few guests watched in horror, George continued to punch Frederick, stopping only when he tired of the inequitable slaughter. The lurid divorce publicity created an even bigger impediment in Frederick's life. When the scandal broke, Frederick's seventeen-year marriage to the former Jennie Hopper, a daughter of Standard Oil magnate George Hopper, ended when Jennie sued for divorce.

Neither George nor Nonnie spent much time grieving over their lost love. Two weeks after the finalization of his divorce, George married the widow Lavina

Pinkley, a former Clevelander now living in Chicago. After Nonnie filed for divorce, George relocated to Chicago, obtained a job in a sporting goods store and courted Lavina. The couple decided to move up their wedding plans when Lavina required surgery that threatened her life. After her successful surgery, the couple faded from the Cleveland scene; George lived to be seventy-eight before his death in 1950.

Nonnie also wasted little time in remarrying, but not to Frederick. She chose instead William Batemann Leeds, one of the richest men in the United States. Attended by a small number of invited guests, the ceremony took place in her parents' Euclid Avenue home near East Eighty-third Street. The groom spent $500,000 on

Lavina Pinkley, George Ely Worthington's second wife, married him shortly after he obtained a divorce from Nonnie May Stewart. *Courtesy of the Plain Dealer.*

wedding gifts, but that amounted to only half of what he paid his former wife of seventeen years to divorce him. She consented after obtaining a million-dollar payoff. William married Nonnie just three days after the finalization of his divorce. As a special added present, he presented his new wife with a yacht and the keys to Rough Point, the former Newport estate of F.W. Vanderbilt.

Originally a florist, William entered the railroad business and purchased a tinplate company in his hometown of Richmond, Indiana. A substantial inheritance given to his former wife helped him launch his career in tin. He and his partners expanded the business, capitalizing on new U.S. tariffs that lessened competition from more established European businesses. William eventually became known as America's "tin king." After her divorce, William's first wife made public appearances at the same events and parties attended by Nonnie, apparently attempting to upstage the new Mrs. Leeds with her own lavish collection of jewels and gowns.

Nonnie and William lived extravagant lives, owning homes in Chicago and on Fifth Avenue in New York City. On a visit to Paris, William bought Nonnie a necklace said to be valued at $200,000. She later engaged in a celebrated battle with the Treasury Department over the appraised value and taxes due when she returned to the United States with the valuable necklace.

Although happily married, William consistently worked long, hard hours. After suffering two strokes, he visited Paris to consult a specialist. Later returning to Paris to regain his health, he experienced a fatal stroke and died at the palatial Hotel Ritz just one day before his planned return to the United States. Not yet forty-seven years old, William left Nonnie an estate worth about $29 million.

American society referred to her as the "tin plate heiress," and in Europe she became the "golden widow." But during the First World War, Nonnie worked actively in relief efforts on both sides of the Atlantic; these efforts changed her identity to the "iron lady." A divorcée and widow by the age of thirty, Nonnie returned to Europe to socialize among the aristocrats. At one of the gatherings, she met Prince Christopher of Greece and Denmark. The prince, dazzled by her beautiful blue eyes, brown hair, pleasant personality and great wealth, soon proposed to Nonnie. The couple remained engaged for six years until they finally married in 1920 after the royal family's opposition to the prince marrying a twice-wed American subsided.

Nonnie joined the Greek Orthodox Church and became Princess Anastasia of Greece. A year after her wedding, her son, William B. Leeds, married eighteen-year-old Princess Xenia of Russia, a union that ended in divorce nine years later. Tragically, Nonnie's marriage to Prince Christopher endured only half as long as their engagement; she died of cancer in 1923.

Meanwhile, following his divorce from Jennie Hopper, Frederick Nicholas became engaged to Florence Mae Murphy, a Euclid Avenue socialite whose father sold tools, fittings, pipes and other supplies in a business located in the Flats. Educated in Cleveland's finest private schools, Florence attended all the most proper parties and balls. The union between Frederick, an excellent singer, and Florence, herself a fine soprano, appeared to be an ideal match almost made in heaven. But Frederick instead remarried Jennie, reviving and extending their previous union. The two remained together, enjoying winters in Pasadena and outings on golf courses, until Jennie's death. Frederick lived as a widower for five years in the exclusive Wade Park Manor near University Circle. In 1928, at the age of sixty-eight, he married Gertrude K. Grover, a childhood friend.

Chapter 2
Adventures in the Cross Family Bedroom

In the 1870s, shocking bedroom activity in David W. Cross's Euclid Avenue mansion interrupted the millionaire's once-serene life. At the time, the *Plain Dealer* called the escapades "the greatest scandal Cleveland ever saw." Cross, his wife and son, an in-home caregiver and a respected doctor interacted to shape a complex controversy providing a decade's worth of decadent gossip material.

David Cross arrived in Cleveland in 1836 to study law with Thomas Bolton, a Euclid Avenue resident. He met Loraine, his future wife, at the Bolton home; as he scrutinized law books, she often visited Mrs. Bolton. Following a brief courtship, the couple married and lived in a small Euclid Avenue cottage that the two later razed to construct a striking Millionaires' Row mansion.

After completing his studies, the young attorney founded a downtown law firm. He expanded his wealth by operating coal mines and founding the Cleveland Steam Gauge Company, a manufacturer of gauges and spring balances used in industrial operations, steam engines and locomotives. The company's international market encompassed the United States, Mexico, South America and New Zealand.

In the 1830s, Cross served as one of the original officers of the Cleveland Lyceum, a forum for lectures, debates, discussions and exchanges of thoughts. In its first year, the organization's members conversed about the ramifications of admitting Texas as a state and the merits and disadvantages of extending voting rights to women. Cross also enjoyed an active involvement with

In 1889, a Washington's Birthday parade passed the imposing mansion of David W. Cross (the tall structure with the cupola). *Courtesy of Cleveland Public Library, Photograph Collection.*

Leonard Case's Arkites; the group's collections constituted a portion of the original exhibits of the Cleveland Museum of Natural History.

His intellectual activities broadened even further. Based on his experiences as a serious sportsman, Cross wrote the rather distinctively titled book *Fifty Years with the Gun and Rod, Including Tables Showing the Velocity, Distance, Penetration or Effect of Shot, Calculated by Leonard Case, Esq.* Chapter headings included "Wild Goose Shooting," "How to Trap Foxes, Mink and Martin," "The Working Tools of the Craft" and "How to Apply the Knowledge You Have Got to Practical Use."

David, Loraine and Henry L. Cross, their only child, first met Emma Bobbitt in 1873 in the London home of a mutual acquaintance. The following year, Emma took up residence in the Cross home, where she ministered to Loraine during an illness. About the same time, Dr. Xenophon C. Scott arrived in Cleveland and quickly developed both a successful medical practice and a nearly fanatical infatuation with Emma. The doctor called on the caregiver at the Cross mansion as many as twenty-seven times in one week, and the two rode, walked, dined and attended the theater together. When Emma's pregnant condition became obvious, the Cross family initiated and encouraged rumors pointing to Dr. Scott as the father of Emma's child. Mr. and Mrs. Cross prohibited the supposedly scandalous Dr. Scott from entering their home. Emma left town for a period to deliver her baby, who sadly died in its first year.

Several years later, as Dr. Scott's medical practice declined because of his alleged dishonorable behavior, he retaliated by filing a lawsuit against the Cross family and Emma Bobbitt. He maintained Henry had fathered Emma's child and the Cross family had threatened and intimidated him into accepting the responsibility.

During a sensational five-week trial, a Cross family maid shocked Clevelanders by testifying that she had seen Henry and Emma sleeping together numerous times in his bedroom. Housekeepers added their own tidbits of information. One noted Henry and Emma had spent New Year's night of 1876 in the same bedroom. Another reported witnessing Emma visiting the family barn in her nightdress. Servants recounted frequent quarrels between the two. Emma once told Henry that if he did not marry her, she would tell Dr. Scott who had actually fathered her expected child. He replied he could produce plenty of witnesses to contradict her claim by bribing them for only $100. Physical violence arose when Emma accused Henry of being the father. When he denied it, she slapped him in the face; in retaliation, he proceeded to choke her.

Recognizing Henry's rapid fall in stature among Euclid Avenue society, and perhaps attempting to correct the previous wrongdoing to Dr. Scott, Emma testified freely against her previous lover. She told the court Henry had provided her with extremely private lessons in the home's billiard room and that she drank liquor with him in his bedroom. She recalled a September night in 1874 when Henry entered her bedroom with more on his mind than billiards and booze. She testified that Henry told her, "If I did not comply with his wishes, he would tell his mother that I had improper relations with Dr. Scott, and that he would ruin my character. I cried and begged of him to cease, but it was of no avail."

The two ultimately engaged in intercourse on an almost nightly basis. During this period, Emma testified that Henry told her, "When I refused to kiss him in September, he had sworn a solemn oath to possess me, body and soul." When Henry learned of her pregnancy, he told her, "My God, Bobbitt, I believe you are in trouble." Emma claimed Henry consulted with several physicians regarding "getting rid of my unborn child," but the medicine he provided proved ineffective. Henry also contributed three dollars to pay for her consultation with a clairvoyant.

As her pregnancy began to show, David inquired about her condition. On instruction from Henry, she told his father that Dr. Scott had caused the pregnancy. As mounting evidence seemed to implicate Henry in the scandal, Emma described two instances when David intimidated her. On one occasion, he told Emma he would prosecute her if she ever said one word against either himself or his son. In another instance, as he violently shook his fists at Emma, he informed her that she "had better be careful in what you say about my son." Emma concluded her testimony by stating, without any doubt or hesitation, that Henry had fathered her child. She also noted that when she attempted to show Henry the baby, he replied, "Take away the brat or I will knock the head off of it."

Both Emma and Dr. Scott testified that no improper relations had been undertaken between the two. To ensure her good name, Emma wrote to the doctor requesting that he compose a letter asking her to marry him. He replied he could not marry anyone for certain reasons unknown to her. Although the court testimony did not pursue these reasons, he had married Edith Scott in 1878. She died in 1886; in 1894, well after the scandal, he married a second time.

On several occasions during the trial, Judge Burke (the lead attorney for the Cross family) displayed his caustic sense of humor. When Burke offered one witness, a past acquaintance, some cautionary guidance, the witness told Burke he didn't want any of his advice. Burke replied he might need it before he got off the witness stand. In another instance, Burke asked a witness if she had any discussions with Dr. Scott's lawyers. When the witness replied she did not know any of the doctor's lawyers, Burke replied, "You're lucky."

David attended nearly the entire courtroom proceedings, filling three or four tablets with notes. Henry, only an occasional visitor, seldom remained in court for more than an hour at a time. Yet police, acting on a tip, managed to arrest Henry on a charge of carrying a concealed weapon into the courtroom. Expecting to find a hidden pistol, detectives discovered only a large pocketknife with a blade about four to five inches in length. Cross claimed he used the knife to cut tobacco.

Following nearly four weeks of testimony, the jury began its deliberations. A *Plain Dealer* reporter, observing the jury for about a month, provided the following descriptions of the twelve jurors:

Juror 1: A baldheaded man with gray whiskers; he steadily stared at the witness who sat just in front of him.

Juror 2: An old man with a wrinkled face and white hair and whiskers; he shook his head disapprovingly with the presentation of especially shocking testimony.

Juror 3: A man with a brown moustache; he confined his attention to Judge Burke.

Juror 4: A black gentleman; he usually sat with his eyes closed, but giggled at some of the testimony.

Juror 5: A juror who found the court stenographer the most interesting aspect of the trial.

Juror 6: A younger person totally uninterested in the case.

Juror 7: An aged man who once stood up and told Judge Burke that he had previously asked the witness the same question.

Juror 8: An attentive young man; he stretched his neck to not miss a word of the proceedings.

Juror 9: An old man; he scowled at court attendees who coughed or moved their chair.

Juror 10: A man not uncommon except for his fidgeting.

Juror 11: A young person who remained quiet and paid close attention.

Juror 12: A man old enough to be the witnesses' great grandfather.

The jury consumed four days of discussions to exonerate Dr. Scott and award him $4,750 in damages. David Cross and the family's attorneys developed a 1,396-page document delineating courtroom errors in their appeal for a new trial. Six years later, the Ohio Supreme Court upheld the verdict favoring Dr. Scott.

By the time Emma delivered her child, Henry had already proposed to Stella W. Wood, whom he soon married. Prior to the wedding ceremony, Emma threatened to take her child to Miss Wood "to show her what a nice baby Henry had."

David died in 1891; in 1908, Henry dissolved his father's firm. Following a growing trend among Euclid Avenue millionaires, Henry moved to Cleveland Heights as commercial interests continued to alter the street's appearance. Suburban living created a few minor but unanticipated inconveniences. The tradition of a congenial but formal butler greeting guests and later announcing "dinner is served" continued into the suburbs. As the hour of an important dinner hosted by the Cross family approached, the always reliable family butler, Robert Baldwin, could not be found. Other servants welcoming the guests could not duplicate Baldwin's grace and charm.

A call from the Cleveland police solved the mystery of the butler's disappearance. The cook responsible for dinner had asked Baldwin to take a large carving knife into downtown Cleveland for sharpening. Not wanting to create suspicion by displaying such an intimidating instrument, Baldwin placed the knife in his coat pocket, where it cut a hole through the clothing and grazed the butler's hand. A policeman, not familiar with the servants of suburban mansions, observed Baldwin's bloody hand and his transfer of the knife to the other side of his coat. The law officer promptly arrested Baldwin for carrying a concealed weapon. Following dinner, Cross journeyed downtown to attest to his butler's character and actions; the police promptly dropped the charges.

Demolition of the former Euclid Avenue home permitted a builder to begin construction of a five-story office building. In 1910, Cleveland Athletic Club members convinced the builder to add nine additional floors to accommodate the club's relocation. The building still exists although the club disbanded.

Chapter 3

The Four Wives of Dan Hanna

From his first marriage, taking place prior to his twenty-first birthday, to his fourth divorce some thirty-four years later, Daniel Rhodes Hanna created enticing tales of marital disasters that combined mystery, intrigue and downright nastiness.

The son of business tycoon and political mastermind Mark Hanna, Dan fit comfortably into Cleveland's rich society. Although he worked competently in his family's iron ore and coal businesses, his passionate interest in newspapers resulted in his purchase of the *Cleveland Leader*

In 1912, a somewhat rumpled-looking Dan Hanna walked down Euclid Avenue's business district. *Courtesy of Special Collections, Michael Schwartz Library, Cleveland State University*.

Constructed in 1895, Dan Hanna's Euclid Avenue residence eventually became the Art Colony Studio Building, a live-work facility for artists. *Courtesy of Cleveland Public Library, Special Collections.*

and construction of the still-existing downtown Leader Building to house the newspaper's operations.

In 1887, Dan, still legally underage, and (Carrie) May Harrington romantically eloped, keeping their marriage a secret for several months. Dan's mother initially threatened to annul the marriage, but Mark created a place for his son in the M.A. Hanna Company. May, the daughter of a wealthy Cleveland coal entrepreneur, and Dan quickly established themselves as a charming Millionaires' Row society couple. The marriage produced three children, Daniel, Carl and Mark. But financial success, social acclaim and an attractive Euclid Avenue home could not alleviate the pressures leading to their divorce in 1898.

The couple worked out a separation agreement without making public either the cause of their problems or the terms of the settlement. Dan repeated this course during his next three divorces. Officially, May charged

Hanna, an active and accomplished horseman, belonged to most of Cleveland's important social clubs. The interior of his home reflected both elegance and the outdoor atmosphere he enjoyed. *Courtesy of Cleveland Public Library, Special Collections.*

Dan with neglect of duty and extreme cruelty. He moved from their Euclid Avenue home, renting and remodeling the former Prospect Avenue residence of the distinguished Myron T. Herrick, later governor of Ohio and ambassador to France. May obtained the Euclid Avenue residence, an undisclosed amount of alimony (rumored to be $8,000 per year) and custody of the couple's three boys. Dan committed to support, educate and defray all the living expenses of their children while they remained in May's custody.

Dan soon discovered the cost of educating his children would be a very expensive undertaking. May submitted a bill of $9,851.96 to cover her 1900 educational activities, which included travel and tutoring expenses associated with excursions to Paris, London and Rome, along with side trips to Venice, Naples, Vesuvius, Pompeii, Florence, Milan, Genoa, Nice and Monte Carlo. After recovering from the rigors of this summer educational jaunt, May and her sons spent the winter in Palm Beach.

Dan complained that he had few opportunities to visit his children. Furthermore, he believed May's exorbitant travel agenda hindered the children's stability without greatly benefiting their education. With powerful political connections, the Hanna family convinced a court to appoint Mark Hanna, Dan's father, as the guardian of the three children.

A sheriff, attempting to serve May with a restraining order that forbid her from moving the children out of northeast Ohio, could not locate Dan's former wife. The lawman and his deputies thoroughly searched the house, not overlooking the contents of the coal bin. The barn proved equally frustrating, even after the deputies forked over all the hay in the loft. The sheriff accurately concluded, "She has given us the slip."

Dan hired a set of Pinkerton detectives who supposedly learned the timing and details of May's plan to travel to New York, register at the Hotel Savoy under the name Mrs. R.W. Jones and, from there, escape to Europe with the children. Even the ship's name and departure time for the getaway had been discovered. An alleged former Hotel Savoy bellboy, familiar with the staff, temporarily assisted the detectives in watching the hotel employees' every move. Following two days of intense surveillance, the defining moment finally arrived as a bellboy in the lobby announced, "Cab for Mrs. Jones." A heavily concealed female hotel guest entered the vehicle. The diligent detectives followed the taxi through the streets of New York for more than an hour, only to witness the cab's arrival back at the hotel.

The mysterious woman in the taxi turned out to be May's maid from her Euclid Avenue home. A detective hired by May had played the part of the ex-bellboy, acting as an informant but providing bogus information. May had actually arrived in New York on a different day, checked into a competing hotel using a name other than Jones and departed New York at a different time and on an unrelated ship. A detective agency hired by May had concocted the entire deception. By the time Dan fully comprehended the situation, May and the boys had already set sail across the Atlantic to embark on another European educational outing. On their trip, the children actually did meet an English princess and the shah of Persia.

May gained celebrity status as the ship cruised to Europe; crowds welcomed her in Britain and the mainland. She told admirers in Ireland, "I shall not return until my children have attained their majority or I am gray headed. I would go to South Africa or the North Pole, if necessary, to retain possession of my children." But May needed no such extremes to stage her triumphant return to Cleveland. Following a conference with Hanna's attorneys in New York on her arrival back in America, she entered her hometown with full custody of the children.

To most everyone's surprise, May joined Cleveland's political arena as the most active member of the Democratic Women's Party of 15. She nudged the organization toward actively opposing any candidate supported by Mark Hanna. Through her intelligence and hard work, she could have become a serious dilemma for Hanna, but she chose instead to relocate to New York, leasing a home on Madison Avenue.

In 1903, May entered into her second secret marriage when family members objected to her union with millionaire Edmund K. Stallo. Edmund, a lawyer, timber operator and railroad builder, owned residences in New York and Cincinnati, the latter city his hometown. He had previously been married to the daughter of Alexander McDonald, a rich Standard Oil magnate, but she died during the marriage. His first union produced two daughters who, through marriages, became princesses.

After about nine years of marriage, May returned from a European trip to rent an apartment separate from her husband, although both lived in the Waldorf-Astoria. She claimed Edmund had gone through all her money; he even lived in luxurious apartments that she paid for and maintained. He then treated her abusively when she could no longer furnish him with cash. In a final indignity, he stripped off part of her clothing in her own apartment. In 1912, their marriage ended following a separation of several years. At the time of the divorce, she resided on Ford Drive in University Circle, close to her children, while he continued to reside in New York's Waldorf-Astoria Hotel. Stallo later remarried and lived to the age of eighty-six but spent many of those years in poverty.

Dan Hanna's youthful elopement initiated a new tradition in the family. In 1908, young Mark A. Hanna (the son of Dan and May) eloped with Adele Pratt, a member of one of the oldest and most aristocratic families of Elmira, New York. The next year, in a Euclid Avenue home, she gave birth to Marcus Alonzo Hanna III, the great-grandson of Senator Hanna.

At the tender age of nineteen, Carl Hanna, another of Dan's sons, ran off with Grace Leavitt. Carl originally attempted a more conventional marriage; he asked his mother's permission to wed Grace, leave Yale without obtaining a degree and enter the business world. After she turned down each request, the couple married in Canada while he playfully sang, "I'm following in father's footsteps, I'm following the dear old dad." Reminiscent of the previous generation, his mother, May, threatened to seek an annulment. Dan, an accommodating father, created a job for his son in the offices of the M.A. Hanna Company with a beginning salary of ten dollars per week. In time, Dan transferred Carl to the company's ore mines of Duluth to obtain field experience.

Dan's second wife, a descendant of Cleveland's wealthy Gordon family, also grew up among Cleveland's privileged class. Following her social debut, Elizabeth "Daisy" Gordon hosted teas and parties, attended the socially proper races at the Glenville track, demonstrated her skills on golf courses and spent her winters in Europe

Rumors persisted that Daisy would marry Roy York, a childhood friend who later entered the brokerage business in New York. But instead, she developed a compulsive desire to journey to Colorado Springs for health reasons, even though she appeared to be perfectly fit. Major Walter De S. Maud, a dashing British army officer and Englishman of considerable wealth, turned out to be Daisy's major interest in traveling west. Walter represented the interests of a London land syndicate with large holdings in America's West. After their long-distance courtship and marriage, Daisy and

Despite an affectionate beginning, the marriage of Daisy Gordon and Dan Hanna ended in a divorce court. *Courtesy of the* Plain Dealer.

Daisy Gordon and Dan Hanna's wedding ceremony took place in Gordon Park on land once owned by her grandfather. *Courtesy of the* Plain Dealer.

Walter resided in both New York and Cleveland. The marriage, unhappy from the beginning, ended in divorce in fewer than three years.

Daisy and Dan married within two months of her official divorce from Walter. The ceremony took place in a Gordon Park cottage; her grandfather had provided Cleveland with the land to create the park. By this time, Dan had relocated from Euclid Avenue to the rich enclave of Bratenahl.

Ironically, Daisy and May Harrington had been schoolmates and close personal friends. In 1902, the two accidentally met in a corridor of the Waldorf-Astoria. Although they did not speak to each other, both of their faces produced stares described as harsh as stone.

In 1906, Daisy enjoyed an extended stay to Rome; when returning to the United States, she made her home in a luxuriously furnished New York apartment apart from her husband. According to Daisy's mother, the marriage problems all stemmed from Dan's shortcomings as a husband. Close friends believed Dan and Daisy separated because she refused to live among Cleveland's millionaires, desiring instead to conduct her social life in New York City.

At 5:30 p.m. on March 5, 1907, two deputy sheriffs served Dan with a divorce petition as he stepped out of his office in the downtown Perry-

Daisy Gordon, Dan Hanna's second wife, is pictured with their daughter Elizabeth. *Courtesy of Cleveland Public Library, Photograph Collection.*

Payne Building. Daisy charged Dan with gross neglect, abandonment, extreme cruelty and drunkenness. Although not part of the court records, knowledgeable sources called the alimony settlement, estimated at $100,000 annually, to be "liberal in the extreme." Their marriage produced two daughters, Elizabeth and Natalie.

An artist depicted the bizarre coincidental meeting of Dan Hanna and his first three wives in the Waldorf-Astoria Hotel. *Courtesy of the* Plain Dealer.

Within two weeks of the divorce, Daisy sailed to France on an extended outing. Later that year, she married Franklin Pelton, a very rich New York resident who had obtained a divorce from his wife less than a week before marrying Daisy. But Dan moved much faster than Franklin. Obtaining his divorce from Daisy on a Friday, he remained a single man over the weekend before entering into his third marriage on Monday.

Not quite living up to the social standards of Dan's first two marriage partners, Mary Elizabeth Stuart had been previously married to Frank Skelly, the head clerk of Cleveland's Gilsey Hotel on East Ninth Street. Justice William Brown, anxious to embark on a vacation, required less than fifteen minutes to perform the no-frills marriage ceremony. Putting on his hat, he concluded the ceremony by proclaiming, "Well, you're married." The newlyweds spent their honeymoon in Ravenna, Ohio (a small town about forty miles southeast of Cleveland), where Dan owned an elegant summer cottage. He had remodeled the 1817 home, redecorating it with furniture and objects supposedly acquired from a renovation of Buckingham Palace.

In the Palm Room of the Waldorf-Astoria Hotel in 1908, Dan and Mary found themselves, by sheer coincidence, seated in the same dining room with Dan's first two wives and their current husbands, Mr. and Mrs. Pelton and Mr. and Mrs. Stallo.

Dan's third marriage lasted nine years, produced three daughters (Ruth, Charlotte and Mary) and ended in divorce. Mary, who initiated the divorce,

Dan Hanna conveyed a distinguished appearance in this photograph. *Courtesy of Cleveland Public Library, Photograph Collection.*

obtained custody of their three daughters. In the same year as his third divorce, Dan married Mollie Covington, the former wife of John B. Worden, another wealthy Standard Oil executive. Dan and Mollie separated in 1920; he purchased a home in Ossining, New York, while she divided her time between her one-thousand-acre Bonny Brier Farm, located in Stockbridge, Massachusetts, and her old home at Ocean Grove, New Jersey. Their marriage problems became acutely evident when Mollie attempted to visit Dan at Ossining and he locked her out. In her 1921 divorce suit, Mollie charged Dan with cruel and abusive treatment. Shortly after the divorce, a court appointed a guardian for her because of her alleged mental incapacity.

In 1921, Dan Hanna died from kidney failure at the age of fifty-five. He had produced three sons and five daughters by his four failed marriages. Even with large alimony payments, Dan left an estate of $3,426,631.54. During the settlement of the estate, actress June Avis Evans surprised the family by demanding a monthly income of $1,250 for the remainder of her life along with the country home Dan had owned in Yorktown and an assortment of automobiles, horses and jewelry. She contended that about nine months prior to his death, Dan had broken off their engagement and promised her the money, home, horses and material goods. She agreed to an out-of-court settlement rumored to be between $25,000 and $60,000.

Chapter 4

Ellena Topliff's Scandalous Affair

W hen Ellena Topliff, the only child of millionaire Isaac Newton Topliff, sued her husband for divorce, her action initiated an onslaught of litigation creating a wealth of gossip eagerly devoured by Euclid Avenue's high society.

Born in Connecticut in 1833, Isaac relocated to Cleveland in 1879 after selling his carriage factory in Michigan. In his adopted city, Isaac amassed his fortune by founding a company to manufacture carriage hardware and by inventing a lightweight tubular steel component used in building carriage tops. Despite his success,

As an inventor and entrepreneur, Isaac Topliff earned his fortune in the carriage building industry. *Courtesy of Cleveland Public Library, Photograph Collection.*

Isaac Topliff constructed his Euclid Avenue residence about 1885. *Courtesy of Cleveland Public Library, Photograph Collection.*

Isaac must have possessed a slightly quirky personality. Police once arrested him for a rather unusual industrial crime: stealing water from a fire hydrant. His night watchman periodically attached a two-hundred-foot hose to the hydrant, transporting the water into a large tank on the factory property.

Ellena, a bright, charming and strikingly beautiful blond, met handsome William P. Todd (generally known as Will) at the Lake Erie Seminary in Painesville, where she studied and he, a traveling shoe salesman, often conducted business. In 1885, following a romantic courtship, Ellena and Will married. The newlyweds, living with Ellena's parents in their Euclid Avenue home, soon developed into a popular couple by attending the avenue's social events and regularly entertaining the upper crust of the street's society. Will, who previously earned about $2,500 annually, assumed a general manager's position at his father-in-law's business. Isaac paid him $1,500 per year plus 10 percent of the company's profits.

The dream marriage faltered quickly. Seeking a divorce, Ellena claimed her husband's intense jealously incited extreme cruelty and violent abuse, including being severely choked, struck in the face, thrown onto a bed, hit in the eyes with the contents of a glass filled with red wine and called vile names. In a Syracuse hotel, Will injured Ellena by throwing her against a large rocking chair and then beating her head on a wall and holding her down with his knees while striking her and threatening to kill her. Will also menaced her with the threat of bodily harm, or even death, if she filed for a divorce.

At the divorce hearings, Ellena claimed her only acts of indiscretion involved jumping into a hammock with another man and walking about a hotel with a gentleman. She added that Will had entered into frequent intimate relationships with other women in Cleveland, Chicago, Buffalo and Cincinnati. Following the descriptions of Will's abuse, the judge granted her an uncontested divorce without delving into the adultery charges.

During the divorce proceedings, Will accidentally met an old acquaintance, the recently divorced Alfred G. Hathaway, at Rumsey's downtown Turkish bathhouse. Will greeted Alfred with a friendly hello, but Alfred responded by calling him a dirty dog because of his abusive treatment of Ellena. Following some further unpleasant name-calling, Alfred landed a punch to Will's mouth, splitting his lip and knocking him into a chair. He then grabbed Will's neck with his left hand while continually punching him in the face with his right hand. Blood flowed profusely, and large crimson swellings covered both of Will's eyes. The attack continued until Alfred, complaining of sore knuckles, mercifully ended the fight.

Eyewitnesses observed that the very trim Alfred sustained a definite advantage against his overweight opponent. Their commentary should have been fairly reliable since Alfred and Will staged their bathhouse bout entirely in the nude. Pleased with his triumphant first round, Alfred invited Will to a gymnasium to continue their battle, but Will declined his invitation. Talking with reporters after the altercation, Alfred claimed a prominent but unidentified businessman also harbored resentment toward Will because of the marriage scandal. Alfred predicted, "If he gets a chance at him, he will fix him so he will not be able to leave his bed for two weeks, at least."

Following the marriage breakup, Will surprised the Topliff family with a barrage of lawsuits against Ellena's parents. He demanded Isaac pay him $20,000 for back wages and his share of the company's profits. Isaac countered by suing Will for payment on a $6,000 promissory note. The court seemed to agree with both sides, ruling that Isaac produce a total of $14,979.98, which represented the difference between the requested back pay with interest and the payment of the promissory note. Topliff appealed the verdict to the circuit court.

Next, Will lodged a $100,000 suit against Frances Topliff, his former mother-in-law, and John S. Gray, a wealthy Syracuse manufacturer of ladies' fine shoes, a family business founded by his father. Will charged the pair

$100,000

Asked by Will Todd.

Huge Sensation in Bon Ton Society.

Will Todd's $100,000 lawsuit against Frances Topliff and John S. Gray created headlines in Cleveland's newspapers. *Courtesy of the* Plain Dealer.

with alienation of affection, arguing he and Ellena had remained happy together until John appeared on the scene. The *Cleveland Press* explained, "The serpent entered their little Eden in the form of a dashing showman from Syracuse, New York; John S. Gray by name."

Will accused John of flirting with Ellena while the latter visited the Topliff home for five days as a houseguest. After his departure, John continued the romance for two years through mail correspondence and secret meetings arranged by Mrs. Topliff. Will submitted convincing evidence to support his claims, including condemning reports by a private detective and samples of John's amorous letters to Ellena. He claimed Ellena and John had spent thirty days making love in the romantic Thousand Islands region straddling the United States and Canadian borders in New York State. Presented as evidence, Will produced this letter, allegedly from Ellena to John:

> *My darling boy: The letter was there for me this morning, and I want to send one more little note to Chicago. It is pretty hard to think it will be so long before I see you, darling. I don't know how I am going to manage it, for I have just been counting the hours, but, of course, I want you to go. I think you are just the grandest fellow always—always doing something for others.*
>
> *I wish you had given me some idea of how long it will take you and what part of the world you are going to, but you can tell me all about it in your letter tomorrow night, and, darling, you will have to get the letter in a little earlier or I will not get it Thursday, for your Sunday letter did not leave Chicago until Monday morning; and write just as long a letter as you can.*
>
> *You will have to do something to cheer me up because you are going away from me instead of coming to me. I wish I were going with you. I suppose if you do not find him at once, and have to hunt him up, there is no telling when you will be here. I feel blue enough at the thought of your going so far from me, but write to me often, darling, and let me know where you are if you can.*
>
> *Oh! Oh! But I do want to see you. How glad I shall be when these few horrible weeks are over with. Time has surely never moved so slowly, but I will be patient and good, for dearest loves me, and although I can't be with him now, it is a great deal to have this love—only I do want to kiss him and love him a little bit.*
>
> *It is hard for me to keep so much affection all bottled up, but it all belongs to the dearest and I am saving it to pour out on his defenseless head when he comes back here. I shall simply love you to death for there is no one else in all the world that I do love and no one gets my real kisses but darling. So just prepare yourself to be nearly eaten up. I wonder if darling will send me the proofs tomorrow. I think he will. I have never written letters to anyone as I have you, dearest. I never liked to write like this before, but it is a pleasure to write to you because you like to have me, and I feel nearer to you when I am writing to you. Darling, it is really—*

At this point, Will entered the room and seized the letter from Ellena, who bit him on the left hand hard enough to require a physician's care. Will also produced a telegram to the Palmer House in Chicago, sent on the same day he commandeered the letter, with the following message: "Do not write. Letter I wrote found. Look out for him. He is furious. Folks on my side." John countered by claiming that Will's cruel treatment caused Ellena to lose all love for him.

Seven months after the finalization of the divorce, the *Cleveland Press* reported, "Another gin fizz bottle in the Todd-Topliff case was uncorked Wednesday evening. It sizzles some, too." Ellena had married John in her parents' Euclid Avenue home. Only close relatives attended the ceremony in which the two married, without the assistance of attendants, and then relocated to Syracuse. The Topliff family and Will settled all the numerous lawsuits out of court. Ellena lived to be ninety-four before her death in 1961.

Isaac continued to reside on Euclid Avenue until his 1904 death from heart failure, which occurred while visiting Ellena in Syracuse. Years later, after his wife's death, a new building housing an automobile showroom replaced the Topliff home. The building evolved into a huge used-car facility; in the 1950s, "The Big Store" promoted itself as Cleveland's largest indoor used-car showroom.

In 1988, Gallucci's Italian Food Market, displaced by the downtown Gateway project, relocated to the old automobile showroom. Remnants of the building's automotive history remain to this day. A large set of double doors, once an entryway for driving automobiles into the showroom, is now a customer exit to a parking lot. A small balcony where salespeople once finalized automobile deals is currently used as a storage area.

Part II

Tragedies
on the Avenue

Chapter 5

Amasa Stone's Frightful Misfortunes

A s Clara and John Hay approached New York Harbor returning from their 1883 European vacation, a pilot boat delivered the latest newspapers to the steamer. Glancing at a headline, a shocked Clara first learned of her father's death. In large, bold print, the paper proclaimed, "Funeral of Amasa Stone." Stone, one of Cleveland's richest industrialists, had committed suicide a few days earlier.

Born on a Massachusetts farm in 1818, Amasa Stone as a teen apprenticed for three years as a carpenter. He earned $40.00 in his first year, $50.00 in his second and $60.00 in his third. At the age of twenty, he collected $1.23 per day working for a railroad. In his first endcavor in the business world, Stone constructed a home for a client who paid him

Amasa Stone successfully aspired to reach the point where he could live on the interest from his investments. In 1882, his annual interest income had grown to $400,000. *Courtesy of Cleveland Public Library, Photograph Collection.*

In 1858, Amasa Stone built this 6,500-square-foot Italianate villa home. Construction of the exterior required more than 700,000 bricks. *Courtesy of Special Collections, Michael Schwartz Library, Cleveland State University.*

with a note from a manufacturing company. The company promptly failed, and Stone's initial business venture turned into a financial disaster. From this very modest start, he transformed himself into a millionaire.

Stone entered the construction business with his older brother and later worked with his brother-in-law designing bridges. Arriving in Cleveland in 1850, he specialized in constructing bridges and railroads, often partnering with Euclid Avenue neighbor Stillman Witt. Similar to Stone, Witt worked his way into Millionaires' Row from a humble beginning. Born in Massachusetts, the future Euclid Avenue resident launched his transportation career by receiving ten dollars per month paddling a ferryboat across the Hudson River.

Stone and his wife, Julia, lived for about ten years in a home on the future site of the Hollenden Hotel on Superior Avenue. In less than a decade, they had accumulated enough wealth to erect their Italianate villa on Euclid Avenue.

As the Civil War began, Stone presided as either president of or on the board of directors of several railroads. During the war, President Lincoln consulted with him regarding supply and transportation issues. By 1868, Stone's annual income surpassed $70,000; a few years later, he possessed $5 million worth of property. But beginning in 1865, a combination of personal tragedy, business setbacks and deteriorating health extracted a heavy toll that ultimately culminated in his suicide.

While studying at Yale, Stone's only son, Adelbert, combined pleasure swimming with the academic task of performing geological examinations in the Connecticut River. On one of these trips, he apparently suffered cramps and drowned before his fellow students could save him.

Stone acquired a reputation as one of the country's foremost wooden bridge builders. But in the late 1850s, railroad companies started replacing wooden bridges with stronger iron or stone structures. Stone's excellent bridge building reputation abruptly ended on the evening of December 29, 1876. Eleven years earlier, he had designed and built an iron bridge seventy-five feet above the Ashtabula Creek near Ohio's northeast border with Pennsylvania. Stone later described the design as "experimental." Even at the time of construction, some of his most experienced employees questioned the bridge's safety. Joseph Tomlinson, a respected engineer, cautioned Stone about possible stress levels on the trusses. Stone promptly fired him. The project's chief engineer resigned rather than build a bridge that he believed to be dangerous.

On that frightful evening in 1876, two engines pulled the luxurious ten-car Pacific Express across the bridge in harsh blizzard conditions. Battling severe cold, fifty-mile-per-hour wind, two feet of snow and much higher drifts, Daniel McGuire successfully navigated the lead engine, a massive thirty-two-ton piece of machinery named Socrates, across the overpass to solid ground. But the 154-foot-long bridge collapsed before G.D. "Pap" Folsom could pilot to safety the even-heavier second engine, the thirty-

The bridge Amasa Stone designed seventy-five feet above the Ashtabula Creek generated controversy from its initial design. *Courtesy of Special Collections, Michael Schwartz Library, Cleveland State University.*

five-ton Columbia. The engine and the train's ten cars plunged into the icy water below.

The last car, the first to reach the three- to six-foot-deep creek covered with eight inches of ice, crashed at an angle with its rear end sticking into the creek. Water, snow and ice rushed through the smashed end. The second car landed on its side; all its passengers died in the icy water. The remainder of the cars crashed, one on top of the other. Overturned heating stoves and oil lamps created an inferno, spreading quickly among the wooden cars. In less than ten minutes, flames rose from every car. The fire's heat melted ice on the creek, sending even more surging water through the cars. Many passengers not killed in the fall either drowned in freezing water or burned in blazing fires; a few died from both causes.

In almost unimaginable scenes of horror, the catastrophe killed travelers from as far as Rochester and Oakland, along with numerous destinations between the two. A father maneuvered out of a burning car while his wife and daughter remained trapped. "Papa, take me with you," the little girl

The Pacific Express plunged into the Ashtabula Creek as the bridge designed and constructed by Amasa Stone collapsed. *Courtesy of Special Collections, Michael Schwartz Library, Cleveland State University.*

cried; the man returned to die with his family. A woman climbed partway from her car but slipped, crushing her own baby to death in her fall. Another woman, with her legs trapped in the wreckage, cried for someone to cut them off so she could be saved from the spreading fire, but the blaze consumed her before any rescuers could gather the courage and equipment to fulfill her wish.

Steep embankments, piled with heavy snowdrifts on both sides of the creek, severely hindered rescue efforts. The exact number of deaths remains unknown, but the accident killed about 92 of the train's 159 known passengers; 83 died at the crash site, and 9 perished later from injuries. Many others suffered serious injuries. Amazingly, eight passengers escaped without any injury. The following morning, the *Cleveland Leader* reported:

> *The haggard dawn which drove the darkness out of this valley and shadow of death seldom saw a ghastlier sight than what was revealed with the coming of this morning. On either side of the ravine frowned the dark and bare arches from which the treacherous timbers had fallen, while at their base the great heaps of ruins covered the one hundred men, women and children who had so suddenly been called to their death.*

A coroner's inquest preceded an investigation by the state legislature. At the inquest, a master carpenter quoted Charles Collins (the railroad's chief engineer since its inception and the person who ultimately supervised construction of the bridge) as saying, "This is no bridge of mine; that is the President's bridge." A railroad attorney offered this testimony: "The bridge was as strong as could be made, and if God saw fit to lower the temperature and lessen the resistance of the iron, the company could not control His action, and hence were clearly not liable for the results of the catastrophe."

The investigators cited an improper bridge design, the Lake Shore & Michigan Southern Railway's inadequate inspections and possible faulty materials used in the initial bridge construction. Investigators who analyzed the bridge debris discovered misplaced struts, braces not tied together and imperfect bearings. Amasa Stone suffered incredible anguish since he personally designed the bridge, reigned as president of the railroad and used the Cleveland Rolling Mill to obtain much of the materials used to construct the bridge. Stone's brother ran the mill, in which Amasa had a substantial investment.

At the state legislature's proceedings, Stone told the investigators the bridge had been designed to be even stronger that it needed to be. To his dying day, he maintained no flaws existed in either the bridge's design or construction. But he probably knew better.

Charles Collins had inspected the bridge just ten days before the fatal collapse. After providing his testimony, the engineer died from a gunshot wound to his head. Since his wife had gone to Conneaut to visit relatives, the fifty-two-year-old remained dead for three days before being discovered in a macabre setting indicating blood had flowed from his mouth and ears. The coroner conducted no inquest since suicide appeared obvious. George B. Ely, a banker and friend of the engineer, noted, "Collins was an extremely proud man and thought more of his honor than his life." But within two years of his death, rumors circulated suggesting Collins may have been murdered. Later evidence indicated the rumors could be true, but no facts ever connected the death to a specific person.

In 1883, a trio of ironworks that Stone controlled in Chicago, Kansas City and Youngstown all failed in succession, almost paralleling the falling of dominos. Although a financial panic had hindered business activity, Stone blamed their demise on high labor costs: "The unreasonableness of men who are disposed to control capital and demand 30 percent more for their work than that paid by eastern mills." At the same time, ulcer problems prevented Stone from sleeping more than two hours each night.

At about two o'clock in the afternoon of May 11, 1883, Stone summoned his private secretary to give him some instructions regarding business matters. His wife then visited him, urging Stone to try to sleep. She would never see him alive again. At about four o'clock, Julia checked his bedside and discovered her husband had left his bed. When she found the bathroom door locked, the butler climbed over the transom to discover Stone lying facedown with his head and shoulders in the tub and the remainder of his body outside. Near the corpse lay a black-handled Smith & Wesson revolver that had propelled a bullet through his heart. He left no suicide letter.

Stone may not have rested in complete peace. About eight years following his death, Boston spiritualist J. Frank Baxter told a large Cleveland audience that an unnamed man (easily identified as J.H. Wade, a recently deceased Euclid Avenue millionaire) had a message that he needed to deliver to Amasa Stone, his former friend, neighbor and frequent business associate.

In 1901, the Stone family suffered its second tragedy at Yale. Adelbert Stone Hay, the son of John and Clara and the grandson of Amasa, returned to Yale, his alma mater, to participate in a homecoming celebration. He had earned his degree just three years earlier. Educated in Cleveland's finest private schools and an excellent student at Yale, Adelbert looked forward to a very bright future; President McKinley had just chosen him as his assistant secretary. On June 23, he sat on a hotel windowsill to take in a breath of fresh air, fell asleep and plunged sixty feet to the sidewalk. The fall killed him instantly. In a heartbreaking twist of fate, the death occurred within a quarter mile of where his uncle had drowned.

In 1910, wreckers demolished the Stone home. The Higbee Company constructed a four-story department store on the site, soon adding a fifth floor. Beginning in 1931, when Higbee's moved to its Public Square location, the building remained mostly vacant. It later returned to its department store heritage by housing one part of the Sterling Lindner Davis store until it closed in 1968. Today, the structure is an office building.

Chapter 6

Extermination of the Potter Family

E mily Rieger, a professional nurse, raced into James Potter's apartment carrying a quickly prepared antidote of eggs and mustard as she responded to Mrs. Potter's anguished cry for help: "Daddy has given us something for a cough—we are all sick." James Potter Jr., a sixteen-year-old senior at East High School, dashed from his room attempting to telephone a doctor, but he collapsed and died on the stairway. Occupants of the apartment building summoned the police when they heard Mrs. Potter screaming, "Maude, Maude. Help! Help!" But neither nurse Rieger nor Maude Hohman (the family's trusted housekeeper and friend) nor the police could save the four members of the Potter family. Mr. and Mrs. Potter, their son James Jr. and his fourteen-year-old brother Robert all died in agony from drinking cough medicine intentionally laced with a deadly dose of poison.

The Potter family had resided in Cleveland less than three months prior to the tragic evening of January 18, 1928. Natives of Steubenville, the Potters enjoyed an excellent reputation in the steel town of about twenty thousand people located on the Ohio River. James and his wife, Lulu, a descendant of one of the city's oldest and most prominent families, resided in one of Steubenville's finest homes.

Although a director of the Steubenville Union Savings Bank and Trust, Potter accumulated the bulk of his fortune by investing in oil wells and other businesses that steadily added to his wealth. But in 1925, the purchase of a large coal tract in West Virginia ended Potter's winning investment strategy. In fact, his failure to obtain a critical railroad

This Euclid Avenue English manor home became the site of a murder and suicide that resulted in the deaths of four people. *Courtesy of Cleveland Public Library, Photograph Collection.*

connection nearly wiped out his entire fortune. With his little remaining capital, he turned to real estate investments, another disastrous strategy for the once-wealthy banker.

After his financial failures, Potter constructed a few homes for clients in the Steubenville area. One of his customers claimed he had obtained $500 under false pretences. The once prosperous and still socially conscious Potter relocated to Cleveland in 1927 to avoid the disgruntled customer's minor but potentially embarrassing accusations.

In Cleveland, Potter took over operations of a twenty-four-room upscale Euclid Avenue apartment building with the hope of generating an income and securing a residence for his family. Potter managed the one-time residence of millionaire shipbuilder Morris A. Bradley, who retained possession of the home when he moved to Shaker Heights in 1921. The apartment's very respectable tenant list included Mary Elizabeth Higbee, widow of the founder of the Higbee Department Store. Another boarder, psychologist Dr. Ira Alzamon, purportedly fathered a child prodigy who lectured scientific societies before reaching the age of four. Later arrested in New York for practicing medicine without a license, Dr. Alzamon, who had developed a vocational guidance system, offered police who interviewed him free advice about obtaining better vocations.

Potter's financial situation grew even worse during his brief stay in Cleveland. Scraping together the remnants of his once vast fortune, Potter responded to the following newspaper advertisement: "HONEST MEN—with about $2,500 to take over one-half share in a light manufacturing business; profits last year $10,000." M.W. Pyle, a resident of a Euclid Avenue apartment, and John C. Schaefer, who lived on East Fifty-seventh Street, sold Potter an interest in a fictitious towrope business. The most factual part of the ad concerned the annual profits. Each of the con men actually did net about $10,000 annually by duping naïve or desperate persons in Ohio, Pennsylvania and Massachusetts.

FEARING RUIN, FATHER SLAYS WHOLE FAMILY

Once Wealthy Contractor Drinks Poison, Then Gives Potion to Wife, Sons

HAD BEEN INDICTED

Euclid Avenue Man Faced Charge of Converting Home Buyer's Money

Pyle, carrying a small device used to weave hemp ropes, told his intended victims he wanted them to make the ropes since his former partner suffered from a sickness that precluded his further participation in the prospering business. Pyle would handle all the sales responsibilities. In truth, Pyle once did have a partner in a rope business. But Harry Eastwood, convicted of swindling Pyle, now resided in prison. Amazingly, Schaefer and Pyle did have towropes to sell, but they generated far more revenue selling phony partnerships. Within a short time, Potter had lost the remainder of his money.

The morning of the catastrophe, the forty-five-

Shocked Clevelanders learned of the Potter tragedy by this headline in the *Plain Dealer. Courtesy of the* Plain Dealer.

year-old Potter asked his two boys to get haircuts. He handed a letter to Miss Maude Hohman, who had come to Cleveland with the family from Steubenville. He instructed Maude to return the document if she saw him the following morning; otherwise, she should open it.

That evening, James and Lulu took their final walk through the neighborhood. At 10:10 p.m., Potter called his attorney to make one last desperate but unsuccessful effort to quash the Steubenville incident. Forty-five minutes later, the entire family lay dead. Potter began the obliteration of his family by drinking his deadly concoction. In the past, he had created "medicines" to prevent illness within his family. Thus, Lulu, James Jr. and Robert harbored no misgivings about consuming his latest "cough pill" even though none of them suffered any illness. Detectives later found twenty-seven lethal capsules (twelve of potassium cyanide and fifteen of strychnine) stored in the family's medicine cabinet. The next day, Maude discovered her envelope contained five twenty-dollar bills, the last vestiges of Potter's former fortune.

Later that year, federal liquor agents raided Das Deutches Haus, the apartment's exclusive restaurant catering to wealthy executives and city and county politicians. The agents first enjoyed a hearty dinner. When the waiters served beer without even being asked, the agents initiated their raid, seizing eleven barrels of beer and arresting the accommodating staff. Thoroughly enjoying the food, the agents procured second helpings after completing their arrests.

Chapter 7

The Horrifying Suicide of Charles Crumb Jr.

C harles Archibald Crumb succeeded admirably in the dry goods and oil industries and then as a stockbroker. Yet his business career ended in failure and his personal life spiraled into a succession of tragedies culminating in the suicide of his son, who lived long enough to discuss his own imminent tragedy with the family.

Born in 1827, Crumb learned the dry goods business from his father, a successful merchant and farmer in Leonardsville, New York. Married in 1849, he relocated to Cleveland, securing employment in a downtown dry goods store. He and George O. Baslington, a co-worker, soon purchased the company. In 1866, the store's Christmas gift selection featured woolen shawls (some in a paisley design), lace goods, embroidered

Charles Crumb endured the collapse of his business and the suicide of one of his sons. *Courtesy of the* Plain Dealer.

handkerchiefs and a large selection of fabric: black Lyons velvets, Irish poplins, French plaids and cases of bleached cottons. For the economy-minded customer, a good selection of dress goods resided on the store's popular "cheap table."

Baslington's father died before George reached the age of seven. Residing in Massachusetts, he earned his own living in a printing office as a typesetter and proofreader. Baslington arrived in Cleveland in 1848 at the age of sixteen.

In 1869, Crumb and Baslington teamed up a second time; after selling the dry goods store, they entered the oil refining industry. Three years later, the pair sold their refinery to Standard Oil and opened a brokerage house. Their company dealt in stocks, grain and provisions and acted as steamship ticket agents for ships leaving New York for Spain, Italy, France, England, Denmark, Egypt, Holland and Greece. By this time, both partners resided on Millionaires' Row, Crumb just west of East Fifty-fifth Street and Baslington near East Forty-fifth Street.

Crumb also invested in real estate and, along with six other investors (including Euclid Avenue residents Amasa Stone, Dan Eells and Henry Chisholm), helped in founding the King Iron Bridge Company. Interested in politics, Crumb served as a member of Cleveland City Council for four terms.

The Charles Crumb family lived in a comfortable Euclid Avenue home at the time of the tragic death of Charles Crumb Jr. *Courtesy of Cleveland Public Library, Photograph Collection.*

In 1887, their well-respected banking and brokerage firm abruptly collapsed. Speaking from his Euclid Avenue home, Crumb told reporters:

> It was owing to our friends being unable to pay us what they owed and living up to what they agreed to do. We were pushed to the wall by the Chicago wheat panic, but had the assurance of one party that we would be taken care of and we rested easily, relying on what they said until 4 o'clock yesterday afternoon, when their confidence was so shaken by the New York panic, and failures throughout the country, that they went back on us.

Baslington, also commenting from his Millionaires' Row residence, noted: "It was simply caused by our friends not responding to calls for margins and we had to stop until we can catch our breath and arrange matters." Following the collapse of the company, Crumb entered the real estate business. In 1891, he narrowly avoided death when a heavily loaded wagon struck his buggy as he traveled on Superior Avenue near the intersection of West Third Street. The buggy collided with a streetcar, throwing Crumb dangerously close to the trolley's wheels. Although suffering injuries, he survived the accident.

None of these misfortunes could have possibly prepared Crumb for the adversity occurring on August 10, 1892. In the morning of that fateful day, Charles A. Crumb Jr., his twenty-nine-year-old son, journeyed to downtown Cleveland in search of employment. The senior Crumb and a daughter commuted to their jobs while Mrs. Crumb, two other daughters and a son enjoyed a day of summer recreation at the family's cottage in Dover Bay Park (now a part of suburban Bay Village).

Returning from downtown, Crumb's son consumed a piece of bread intentionally laced with a full teaspoon of Rough on Rats poison. Despite the lethal dosage, he remained conscious long enough to discuss his impending death with his father and sister, who had returned home from work. When Charles admitted taking the poison, his sister placed an urgent call to Dr. H.J. Burdick, the family doctor and friend, who arrived in about twenty minutes with a stomach pump. For a short time, Charles's condition seemed to improve, but his health deteriorated as the evening progressed.

Charles claimed his inability to secure employment created his severe despondency. He told his sister, "I am sorry I did it, and really don't know why I was so foolish. I believe I was temporarily insane, for under no other circumstances would I have done it." Later in the evening, Charles told his sister, "I am hungry; please give me some ice." He then seemingly went to sleep and died at 10:45 p.m.

A teaspoon of this readily available household product killed Charles Crumb Jr. *Courtesy of the* Plain Dealer.

The troubled youth had worked as an order clerk in the wholesale department of McIntosh, Huntington & Company. He then found employment with National Carbon, where he worked for only three weeks before resigning due to health concerns. Unmarried, Crumb had spent the majority of his spare time reading literature. At the coroner's inquest, Dr. Burdick offered his view of the tragedy:

> *Crumb was quiet and cared little for company. He seemed despondent because he was out of employment. His income was enough to support*

him with little effort. He had no reason to feel he was a burden on anyone. He never cared for ladies' society and was generally with his mother in the evening. His despondency was caused by disappointment at not being able to progress in his business as rapidly as his associates.

On the morning of September 3, 1894, Charles Crumb Sr. awoke at six o'clock and told his wife he felt unusually well. A half hour later, his wife found him dead at the age of sixty-seven. His home functioned for a short time as an apartment before Edward Polster constructed a new office building on the site. Following the business failure, George Baslington became general manager of the Chapin Bolt and Nut Company. He died in 1899 at the age of sixty-seven.

Chapter 8

Corrigan Family Catastrophes

S teel magnate Captain James Corrigan suffered a tragedy almost too horrifying to comprehend—the drowning deaths of his wife, three daughters, an infant granddaughter and a niece.

Corrigan owned numerous schooners and steamers used in his business enterprises and enjoyed sailing as a recreation. In 1899, he purchased a pleasure yacht named *Idler* and spent about $8,000 to extensively renovate the vessel originally built in 1864. During the holiday Fourth of July week in 1900, James Corrigan, his brother John and members of both families cruised on the *Idler* during a weeklong sailing and fishing outing on Lake Erie, the Detroit and St. Clair Rivers and the St. Clair Flats.

Had James and John remained on board for the entire trip, the terror of July 7, 1900, most likely would not have occurred. As experienced mariners, either one would have successfully navigated the yacht through a fierce sixty-mile-per-hour gale. But long before the storm struck, James and John had departed the yacht in Port Huron, Michigan. James, troubled by an ear problem, traveled to Cleveland by rail to confer with his doctor. John set out for a business meeting in Buffalo. After arriving back in Cleveland before his family, a very alarmed James watched the harbor and intensifying storm from his office window in the Perry-Payne Building. No sign of the *Idler* ever appeared.

When the brutal winds began to pound the yacht, Captain C.H. Holmes strongly recommended all passengers return to the deck, which he perceived as safer than the cabin below. But in a state of terror, most

The year after James Corrigan purchased and renovated the *Idler*, the yacht sank in a Lake Erie windstorm. *Courtesy of the* Plain Dealer.

Right: Crew members nearly saved the life of fifteen-year-old Ida May Corrigan before she vanished into Lake Erie's turbulent waters. *Courtesy of the* Plain Dealer.

Opposite, bottom left: Mrs. John Corrigan, the only passenger to survive the windstorm, clung to a deck couch in the water for about thirty minutes before being rescued. *Courtesy of the* Plain Dealer.

Opposite, bottom right: Brave Etta Corrigan drowned attempting to save members of her family. *Courtesy of the* Plain Dealer.

of the passengers remained beneath the deck. Only Mrs. John Corrigan and Ida May Corrigan, her fifteen-year-old niece, abandoned the doomed cabin. The *Idler* keeled on its side about sixteen miles from Cleveland. Etta Corrigan, the eighteen-year-old daughter of Mrs. John Corrigan on vacation from Vassar College, climbed to the deck and helped place her mother on a floating deck couch. The only passenger to elude death, Mrs. Corrigan battled the waves while clinging to the couch for about thirty minutes. She then suffered bruises to her face and hands when struck by a tug attempting a rescue. The crew eventually pulled her out of the water, saving her life. Meanwhile, Etta returned to the cabin, apparently in a futile attempt to retrieve other passengers.

As the storm strengthened, Ida May desperately clung to the side of the yacht. A sailor on the *Idler* grabbed her when a line from a passing fishing tug was thrown on deck. He wound the rope around his arm while holding Ida May. But when the crew of the tug drew the line to pull the two to safety, it jerked the sailor's arm, forcing him to let go of Ida May, who disappeared into Lake Erie's towering waves. Seven weeks later, a crew member of the steamer *City of Detroit* retrieved her badly decomposed body floating in the lake.

Another crew member held twenty-year-old Jane Corrigan in the water for a minute before she slipped from his grasp. Nearly three

Left: A sailor lost his grip on Jane Corrigan, sending the twenty-year-old to her death. *Courtesy of the Plain Dealer.*

Below: Divers used the *T.C. Lutz* tugboat as a base to search for the Corrigan families' drowned bodies. *Courtesy of* Cleveland Press.

months after the tragedy, a fisherman discovered her body washed ashore near Willoughby.

The *Idler* sank to the bottom of Lake Erie. After the lake calmed, divers from the tug *T.C. Lutz* searched for the remains of the two families. To provide up-to-the-minute news bulletins of their progress, the *Cleveland*

Right, top: Mrs. James Corrigan drowned wearing a life preserver and expensive jewelry. *Courtesy of the* Plain Dealer.

Right, bottom: Mrs. Charles Rieley and her infant daughter both died in the tragic sinking of James Corrigan's yacht. *Courtesy of the* Plain Dealer.

Press dispatched a reporter, an owner of carrier pigeons and a dozen of his most robust birds to accompany the crew of the *Lutz*. The divers recovered three bodies on the first day of their gruesome hunt. From her facial expression and position within the vessel, the searchers concluded forty-eight-year-old Mrs. James Corrigan may have made a frantic effort to reach the upper deck, but water filled the cabin too quickly for her to survive. Still wearing a life preserver, her diamonds and jewelry remained perfectly in place.

Mrs. Charles Rieley (the twenty-two-year-old daughter of James Corrigan) died attempting to clutch Mary Corrigan Rieley, her one-year-old baby. In death, a life preserver still dangled from

the mother's waist. The divers also retrieved the body of the gallant Miss Etta Corrigan. Within a few days, they discovered the body of the infant Mary Rieley, previously hidden from view by furniture. Much later, retrieval of the bodies of

Millionaire James Corrigan lost most of his immediate family in a horrible boating accident. *Courtesy of Cleveland Public Library, Photograph Collection.*

Ida May and Jane completed the horrifying search.

None of the yacht's crew died, although crew members used lifeboats to save Captain Holmes, who had been washed overboard. James Corrigan blamed the accident entirely on the carelessness of Captain Holmes; John added he believed the *Idler* could have sailed across the Atlantic Ocean. Although he was later exonerated, police initially arrested Captain Holmes for manslaughter.

Meanwhile, as the Corrigan family mourned their dead, a household maid stole clothing and other personal items belonging to the then still-missing Jane Corrigan. Adding to the family miseries, a Russian sailor, hired by Corrigan to assist in raising the *Idler*, first looted the cabin of $10,000 worth of jewelry and diamonds. As time passed, members of the Corrigan family both incurred and inflicted further personal tragedies.

Born in 1849 in Oswego, New York, James Corrigan launched his sailing profession as a runaway on a Great Lakes ship. During his lifetime, he mounted separate businesses in oil, lake shipping and iron. He entered the refining business and created processes for efficiently manufacturing mineral and machine oil. He began with a very small refinery on Cleveland's south side that grew rapidly in size. In 1881, Corrigan's childhood friend John D. Rockefeller purchased his oil interests for three thousand shares of Standard Oil stock, more than enough to make Corrigan wealthy.

After working for a few years to establish oil refineries in Austria, Corrigan borrowed money from Rockefeller to enter the Great Lakes shipping business. When Corrigan purchased iron mines near Lake Superior, he turned again to Rockefeller, who supplied additional money using Corrigan's Standard Oil stock and mortgages on shipping vessels as collateral. Rockefeller also

Above: In 1907, James Corrigan constructed a nineteen-room residence on Euclid Avenue. The next year, he died in the home. *Courtesy of Cleveland Public Library, Photograph Collection.*

Right: The inheritance of playboy James Corrigan Jr. initiated a new chapter in the family's tragedies. *Courtesy of Cleveland Public Library, Photograph Collection.*

assumed a bank loan Corrigan had obtained by using the remainder of his Standard Oil stock as security. In 1890, when Corrigan failed to pay the interest on his loans, Rockefeller foreclosed, gaining back all of Corrigan's Standard Oil stock but ending their friendship. Corrigan sued Rockefeller, claiming the oil tycoon had misrepresented the price of the stock when he reacquired it. Through appeals, the case worked its way to the U.S. Supreme Court; Corrigan lost the original suit and every one of the appeals.

In 1894, Price McKinney joined Corrigan's firm as a partner. His management skills rejuvenated the company, which had suffered through the harsh 1893 recession. In recognition of his work, Corrigan changed the company name to Corrigan, McKinney & Company.

In 1908, James Corrigan died of appendicitis in his Euclid Avenue home. At the time of his death, he headed the mining company as well as presiding over five shipping companies and four other mining concerns. Fun-loving James W. Corrigan Jr., known to the family as Jim or Jimmy, inherited 40 percent of his prosperous father's company and a substantial amount of cash. But his father, not trusting Jimmy with the family fortune, provided him with only $15,000 in cash and appointed Price McKinney as a trustee to control Jimmy's wealth until he reached the age of forty, but only if McKinney considered Jimmy mature enough to control his inheritance in a wise manner. Otherwise, McKinney would continue as trustee. McKinney also received a 30 percent stock interest of his own; he thus controlled the bulk of the company stock.

James Corrigan Sr. seemed to exercise sound judgment in establishing the trust. By the time his son—born in 1880 in Austria, where his father had built oil refineries—reached the age of thirty, he played centerfield and managed the Spinks, one of northeast Ohio's best amateur baseball teams, and owned racehorses in Kentucky. The year following his father's death, Miss Georgia Young of Pittsburgh sued Jimmy for $50,000, claiming breach of promise when he ended their marriage engagement. Few people who knew Jimmy believed he had the ability to run a major business. Yet within a few years, Jimmy would marry into all the maturity he needed to gain control of his father's former company.

On December 2, 1916, Corrigan married Laura Mae MacMartin, whom he originally met at his father's funeral. His Wisconsin-born wife—the daughter of handyman Charles Whitlock and his wife, Emma—had previously married Duncan R. MacMartin, a hotel doctor. James's playboy reputation and his marriage to a divorcée from a working-class background led Cleveland's best families to shun the pair and defeat Laura's efforts to enter local society. The equally unimpressed McKinney reorganized the

Laura Mae Corrigan, the widow of James Corrigan Jr., became a foremost European society hostesses. *Courtesy of Cleveland Public Library, Photograph Collection.*

company as a corporation and renamed it McKinney Steel, eliminating the Corrigan name.

The newlyweds didn't fare much better among the social elite in New York City, but in Europe, Laura Mae soon developed into one of London's leading society hostesses. Even while residing in Europe, Laura Mae and Jimmy bore a continuing resentment toward Price McKinney, who still controlled Jimmy's money. Laura Mae convinced the heirs of Stevenson Burke, the elder Corrigan's original partner, to sell their 13 percent interest in the company to Jimmy. Through bitter courtrooms battles, she helped her husband gain control of his 40 percent interest formally held in McKinney's trust. Jimmy, now owning 53 percent of the company stock, returned to Cleveland in 1925 to attend a stockholders' meeting. The surprised group witnessed Jimmy's announcement that he now controlled enough stock to hold majority ownership, his firing of Price McKinney and his restoration of the company name Corrigan-McKinney. Before the year ended, a despondent McKinney fired a bullet through his head.

Jimmy demonstrated he could act decisively when the circumstances demanded quick action. While Jimmy and Laura Mae enjoyed one of their international tours, he received notice that Michael Dugan, his secretary and confidential clerk, had embezzled nearly $150,000 of the couple's money. Jimmy raced back to Cleveland in enough time to catch Dugan, who received a two-year prison term. But within three years of Jimmy's business takeover, he suffered a fatal heart attack in front of the Cleveland Athletic Club on Euclid Avenue. Laura Mae transformed her inheritance into an annuity paying her an annual income of $800,000; she continued to reside in Europe.

As World War II spread to Paris, the U.S. government froze her funds, leaving her with a $500-per-month allowance. She sold her jewelry, tapestries and furniture to finance wartime relief efforts. Dwindling finances sent Laura Mae, now called the "American Angel," back to London in 1942, where she established the Wings Club for aviators. While visiting her sister in New York, Laura Mae died on January 22, 1948, thus concluding the tribulations of two generations of the Corrigan family.

Part III

Bending and Breaking the Law

Chapter 9

The Search for Josie Blann

Josephine Blann, allegedly of unsound mind, resided on Euclid Avenue with her mother, Percis, and stepfather, Abraham. The family never fit into the Millionaires' Row society, mostly because of persisting gossip involving Abraham's source of wealth. Prior to the Civil War, he had opened and quickly closed a dancing school where couples learned to waltz for six dollars a lesson. He then sold a folding clothes dryer apparatus that did not attain overwhelming acceptance. Yet after the war, Abraham had accumulated enough money to construct a fashionable Euclid Avenue home. His neighbors believed he had acquired his wealth by continuing an unprincipled cycle of collecting a substantial bonus payment for enlisting in the army during the war and then deserting the troops, only to receive another bonus for reenlisting using an assumed name.

The supposedly simple-minded Josie owned about $40,000 worth of property, an amount guaranteed to increase substantially when she inherited the home her parents had already deeded to her. But Abraham soon decided Josie did not possess the capabilities to care for her parents, the home or even herself. Josie's mother and stepfather persuaded her to deed the property to William J. Grand, an individual previously unknown to the family. He agreed to take care of Percis, Abraham and Josie during their lifetimes in exchange for Josie's property. Soon believing Grand had obtained the property in a fraudulent manner, the family initiated a lawsuit to prevent him from selling their home. May Harter, a twenty-one-year-old married niece of Josie residing in New York, demanded Josie regain

$10 A DAY!

AGENTS WANTED,

For the sale of TIFT'S PORTABLE

Folding Clothes Dryer,

Patented July 20, 1858.

THIS IS AN ARTICLE THAT NO WOMAN will do without after once seeing, and one which no active Agent can make less than TEN DOLLARS A DAY net profit. The retail price is only $4, and an intelligent Agent never fails in selling at least ten Dryers to every twelve Families—consequently those purchasing County Rights will buy Fortunes. YOUR CHANCE IS GOOD until the rights are all sold.

Call at 188 Ontario street, or 24 Howe street and learn particulars.

Or address, post-paid, L. J. ADAMS or A W. BLANN, Cleveland, Ohio.

In 1859, Abraham Blann sought agents to sell his folding clothes dryer. *Courtesy of the Plain Dealer.*

Opposite: Abraham Blann constructed his Victorian villa home on the Euclid Avenue site of a former Civil War soldier camp. *Courtesy of Special Collections, Michael Schwartz Library, Cleveland State University.*

control of her estate. An agreeable judge annulled the transfer of the property to Grand.

When Josie's stepfather died, a judge appointed Perry Prentiss as the guardian of Percis even before Abraham's corpse could be removed from the house. Purportedly at the insistence of May Harter and without any formal examination, the judge declared Percis an imbecile and Josie an idiot. Prentiss then served as Josie's guardian as well.

Following her stepfather's death, Josie and her widowed mother frequently visited and sometimes even lived in the Euclid Avenue home of Mrs. Josephine Ammon, a family friend. In 1863, Colonel John Henry Ammon,

The year following construction of their Euclid Avenue home (right), Mrs. Josephine Ammon divorced her husband. *Courtesy of Cleveland Public Library, Photograph Collection.*

a Civil War participant and once traveling salesman for *Harper's Magazine*, had married the former Josephine Mary Saxton, then a nineteen-year-old Cleveland resident. John returned to the Civil War battlefront almost immediately after the wedding ceremony. When the conflict ended, and with no tie to Cleveland other than his wife, John launched a successful career in book publishing while residing in Chicago, New York and Boston; Mrs. Ammon chose to remain in Cleveland. The year after the completion of their Millionaires' Row home, she divorced John, claiming desertion and gross neglect.

Mrs. Ammon continued to live in her Euclid Avenue residence after acquiring a generous divorce settlement from John and a sizeable estate from her father, who had earned a comfortable living as a surveyor, farmer and real estate investor. Along with managing a thirty-acre vineyard to supply grapes to hotels and other businesses, Mrs. Ammon devoted considerable time and effort to establishing and supporting Cleveland charities.

Seemingly off-beat peculiarities often arose in Mrs. Ammon's life. Once when she was suffering from an acute water shortage on her farm, the exact spot of a vast supply of water appeared to Mrs. Ammon in a dream. The following morning, she directed one of her workmen to the location, instructing him to start digging. Much to his amazement, he discovered an abandoned stone well and spring; the combination soon supplied the farm with an abundant supply of water.

Mrs. Ammon agreed to act as guardian to both Josie and Percis Blann, even inviting them to live with her. She also petitioned the court to remove Prentiss as the pair's legal guardian. In addition, Mrs. Ammon noted that friends of Josie and Percis, along with several doctors, believed the two to be perfectly sane. The judge removed Prentiss as guardian but replaced him with Thompson H. Johnson, a relative of May Harter.

Percis, nearing death, asked Judge Daniel Tilden for assurance that Josie would remain with Mrs. Ammon. He responded with the following letter:

> *Mrs. Blann: I have heard this morning that you wish some statement from me giving you the assurance that Josie shall not be removed out of the jurisdiction of the probate court of this county or that in case of your death she shall not be removed from where she now is until the business of the case between her and her present guardian is fully settled. I promise all this. Yours Truly, Daniel R. Tilden.*

On Percis's deathbed, Mrs. Ammon promised to care for Josie. When Johnson arrived to assume custody of Josie and her coveted estate, Mrs. Ammon claimed she had no idea of her whereabouts. She told the sheriff, "Josie walked out that front door of her own free will, and I have not seen her since. Her mother told her before she died to run away and hide rather than get into Johnson's hands."

Authorities searched both Mrs. Ammon's Euclid Avenue home, from attic to basement, and her summer residence in Collinwood but failed to uncover the missing Miss Blann. Based on a tip, deputies also searched the home of Mrs. George G. (Margaret) Colgrove, a first cousin of Percis, also to no avail. Mrs. Colgrove claimed all she knew about Josie could be found in the newspapers. Meanwhile, a collection of Josie's long-lost relatives throughout the country claimed their right to take care of her and ultimately inherit her property.

In court, Mrs. Ammon testified that although she did not know the whereabouts of Miss Blann, she did have "an idea" regarding where Josie may have fled. After she refused to divulge the details of her theory, the judge sentenced Mrs. Ammon to prison for contempt of court, where she would remain until she disclosed the particulars of her idea. Mrs. Ammon explained to a *Plain Dealer* reporter, "An idea is a random thought, while an opinion is an accumulation of ideas. An idea is a good ways from a fact. How long would a judge hold one on the witness stand who simply has an opinion formed from ideas? I have an idea that, if I put all my wits together, I could find her." For the remainder of her life, Mrs. Ammon claimed uniqueness as the only woman ever incarcerated for possessing an idea.

The martyrdom of Josephine Ammon, a woman of means and social position, generated national publicity. Preparing for a long imprisonment, Mrs. Ammon moved her bed, several chairs, a rug and numerous books and pictures from her Euclid Avenue mansion to her new residence in the Cuyahoga County jail. Hundreds of friends and sympathizers flocked to her Public Square cell to demonstrate their support and scrutinize her luxurious cubicle. Well-wishers brought flowers and food, although Ammon praised the jail's excellent bean soup, often inviting her society friends to enjoy the unconventional cuisine with her.

After forty-one days, the novelty of lavish imprisonment waned. Ammon finally revealed Josie's hiding place, a farmhouse in Geauga County where friends told Josie to hide in the hay if anyone tried to search the house. Two of her friends brought her safely back to Cleveland. Josie testified that she hid to save her life, believing Johnson would poison her to obtain the estate.

When learning she would be placed in the care of Mr. Johnson, Josie became so emotionally excited that the judge placed her in his private room. To witness the events, Mrs. Ammon ran out of the courtroom, down the corridor and through the law library to reach the judge's chambers. Johnson prevented Mrs. Ammon from entering, physically throwing her back. As Johnson restrained Mrs. Ammon, the judge arrived, closed the door and then let Johnson enter.

Sobbing hysterically, Josie cried, "I don't want him. No, I don't want him. He will kill me. He will poison me. They want to rob me. He's guardian over me. I know all about it…Oh! Oh! Let me go. I don't want him." This scene constituted the first meeting between Johnson and Josie. She broke away and ran down the hall. Eventually restrained, Josie spent the night in the home of Dr. Chauncey J. Keeler, the Blann family physician for more than thirty years. The doctor predicted Josie would need ten days to recover before the hearing could continue.

In a subsequent court hearing, attorneys for Johnson used the William J. Grand incident as practical evidence that Josie could not handle her own affairs. A judge had nullified Grand's arrangement mainly because he believed Josie to be an imbecile when she entered into the agreement. If Josie could be trusted to competently manage her affairs, then she had regained her property from Grand in an unlawful manner. Finally, a new probate judge ended the case by placing Josie in the custody of a trustworthy family while allowing her property to remain in the charge of Johnson.

Although Mrs. Ammon lived in relative comfort during her incarceration, she observed the quandaries of others not as fortunate. The experience inspired her to work toward prison reform. She visited the Ohio State Penitentiary several times, suggested changes to improve conditions of the prisoners and frequently presented lectures at the penitentiary. Never one to discourage an unconventional view of life's experiences, she also constructed a replica of her jail cell in her Euclid Avenue home.

In 1892, at the age of forty-eight, Mrs. Ammon died in her Euclid Avenue home. More than one thousand people, including newspaper reporters, attended her funeral, all invited by Mrs. Ammon before she died. Laid to rest in Lake View Cemetery, she had selected a final resting place southwest of the Garfield Monument because she perceived it as wild, unconventional and romantic.

For the remainder of her life, Josie staged unsuccessful legal battles to regain control of her assets. Following Josie's death from cancer in 1900, Dr. Edward Harvey Cushing, one of the family's five generations of esteemed doctors, purchased the home. In 1917, the Cushing family moved to Bratenahl. Within a few years, the home and surrounding parcels had all been consumed by new or used car lots. In 2010, an office building replaced the automotive lots that once engulfed the Blann home.

Chapter 10

The Doctor and the Swindler

When Dr. Leroy Chadwick's father discovered oil on his Pennsylvania farm property, he sold the land, relocated to Cleveland and constructed a home on Euclid Avenue. Leroy led an exemplary life; he neither drank nor smoked nor chewed tobacco. Yet in 1904, as he returned from Europe on the steamship *Pretoria*, sheriffs from multiple states waited at New York Harbor to serve him with arrest warrants. The doctor had inadvertently become a party to one of America's most sensational swindling schemes.

In 1882, Dr. Chadwick married Martha Heward. The couple prospered financially by combining his lucrative medical practice income with astute real estate investments. Martha became one of Euclid Avenue's finest society women. When, in 1894, she tragically died at the age of thirty-eight, Dr. Chadwick occasionally frequented a West Twenty-fifth Street brothel. Here he met Cassie Hoover, the madam who promoted her business as a boardinghouse for "refined young women," most of whom doubled as prostitutes. Cassie's upscale whorehouse provided her with monthly rent (essentially commissions from prostitution fees) and the blackmail she extorted from some of Cleveland's most prominent male citizens.

The madam and the doctor quickly entered into their own romantic relationship. An acquaintance warned Dr. Chadwick not to rush into his planned marriage since rumors persisted that Cassie possessed a "bad record." But the doctor viewed his future bride as "a most honorable lady." Unfortunately, Chadwick should have heeded what turned out to be excellent advice.

Above: During the Civil War, Dr. Leroy Chadwick's father constructed this sixteen-room brick home on Euclid Avenue. *Courtesy of Cleveland Public Library, Photograph Collection.*

Right: Cassie Chadwick highlighted her outlandish criminal career by defrauding several banks out of millions of dollars. *Courtesy of Cleveland Public Library, Photograph Collection.*

Born in Ontario, Canada, in 1857, Elizabeth Bigley (Cassie's real name) launched her bizarre criminal career at the age of thirteen. Arrested for passing bad checks, police released Elizabeth to the custody of her parents. Two years later, after a $5,000 check bounced, a judge acquitted her due to temporary insanity. Relocating to Toronto, she received a second exoneration for passing bad checks because of her mental condition.

Elizabeth relocated to Cleveland, living with her sister and brother-in-law on Franklin Avenue. One day, she offered to babysit for the couple so they could enjoy an evening to themselves. While they attended a vaudeville show, Elizabeth invited at least two (and possibly as many as four) mortgage companies to inspect the home's furniture. Using these possessions as collateral, she received cash payments for the mortgaged furnishings. Elizabeth found a new home and invented a new name before the first payment notice arrived at her sister's residence.

Now known as widowed Lydia DeVere, in 1882 she married Dr. Wallace S. Springsteen, a physician and former Civil War hero who had engaged in fifteen separate battles within a two-year period. Their hasty marriage is partially explained by Lydia's tale of being next in line to inherit a large castle in Ireland, an event that would turn the doctor into a very wealthy husband. If their marriage took place quickly, the subsequent divorce occurred with even greater rapidity. After learning of her dubious past activities, Wallace started divorce proceedings after a marriage of eleven days. In their short period of marital bliss, Lydia had already run up substantial bills to merchants. When a newspaper published her wedding photograph, her numerous creditors learned how to press charges against the former Elizabeth Bigley. The doctor chose to honor her debts, even though he lost everything he owned; creditors even seized his stethoscope.

Although not exerting much power over Lydia in his lifetime, Dr. Springsteen seemed to acquire a strange force some thirteen years following his death. Clairvoyant Mrs. M. Lane (not in any way related to Cassie) claimed she had developed grand cures for illness while under the influence of the doctor's departed spirit. The inspirations did not stop police from charging Mrs. Lane with practicing medicine without a license.

The future Cassie Chadwick next surfaced as Madam Marie LaRose, a clairvoyant. In 1883, she married one of her clients, John R. Scott, a Trumbull County farmer. Four years later, she confessed to adultery in a successful effort to end the boring marriage. Given her motivations for earlier and later marriages, the logic of the Scott affair remains a mystery. In any case, she returned to Cleveland as clairvoyant Lydia Scott, a name she soon changed back to Madam Lydia DeVere. She married C.L. Hoover; this marriage produced her only offspring, a son named Emil. Hoover died within two years of the marriage, leaving her an estate worth about $50,000.

The widow Hoover surfaced briefly in Buffalo, posing as the ailing wife of a rich man who owned gold mines in China. She graciously arranged for her new friends to invest in these fictitious mines. Returning to Ohio, she moved to Toledo as the reincarnated clairvoyant Madam DeVere. Seeking another gullible man, she portrayed herself as either the daughter of a British general who would soon be receiving large amounts of money, the widow of an earl or the niece of President Ulysses S. Grant.

Next she transformed herself into the real-life Florida G. Blythe, owner of valuable real estate properties in Cleveland. Cassie's fabricated version of Florida had acquired notes supposedly signed by Richard Brown, another authentic person with considerable wealth and even richer business contacts. An impressionable Joseph Lamb, well known in Toledo as a man with a sterling reputation for integrity, asked Florida to act as his financial advisor. Joseph gladly cosigned and cashed Florida's notes from Richard Brown, saving her the inconvenience of returning to Cleveland each time she needed money.

When the checks bounced, police arrested both Joseph and Florida. A jury, viewing Joseph as a helpless victim of Florida's complete dominance, possibly even to the point of hypnosis, acquitted him. He died within a short time of this exploitation. Again posing as Madam DeVere, Cassie spent three and a half years in a Toledo jail for forgery before receiving a parole. While confined in prison, she predicted that the prison warden would lose $5,000 in a failed Cincinnati business deal and then die of cancer. Both of her prophesies proved amazingly accurate.

Paroled from prison, she returned to Cleveland using the name Cassie L. Hoover. She met Dr. Chadwick in her collective boarding home and brothel on West Twenty-fifth Street. Cassie told the doctor she had just started managing the boarding home and professed complete surprise that prostitutes frequented the stylish establishment. She knew she must leave this horrid environment immediately but had not yet earned the money needed to rent a more suitable place. The benevolent Dr. Chadwick invited Cassie to temporarily live in his Euclid Avenue home with his mother and sister. As an unexpected perk, the doctor discovered that Cassie could help alleviate his pain from rheumatism by administrating evening massages in his bedroom. Within a short time, Dr. Chadwick proposed marriage, and Cassie willingly accepted. Shortly afterward, Leroy's mother died, and his sister departed to live with her brother in Pennsylvania.

Dr. Chadwick's comfortable residence provided a perfect setting to unleash Cassie Chadwick's creative mind. *Courtesy of Cleveland Public Library, Photograph Collection.*

On Christmas Eve 1897, soon after their wedding, Cassie and Leroy enjoyed a performance of *A Stranger in New York* at the Euclid Avenue Opera House. Upon their return home, the doctor must have felt akin to a stranger in his own house. Without his knowledge, Cassie had purchased completely new furnishings, replacing virtually every piece of the home's former high-priced but dull decor. She arranged to have her new motif delivered as a Christmas present for Leroy while the two attended the show.

Among handsomely carved furniture and expensive oil paintings, Cassie's new selections included a pink sofa in the shape of a seashell and a chair that played music when an unsuspecting guest sat on it. Persian rugs covered the floors, and a $9,000 pipe organ graced the music room. Ruby-encrusted silverware and soup plates, fitted atop music boxes, adorned her new dinner table. Cassie's pristine jewelry chest contained eight trays of diamonds and pearls valued at $98,000.

Although Cassie took great pleasure in her new furnishings, she concocted the scheme for a different reason. Knowing nothing of her background or pedigree, her wealthy neighbors had acted rather aloof. But the movers, decorators and painters arriving on Christmas Eve created an almost irresistible curiosity among her neighbors and acted as a very effective icebreaker. Both Cassie and the home soon became the personification of wealth, luxury, excessiveness and hospitality.

Cassie willingly shared her supposed wealth with her friends, employees and even a few casual acquaintances. Her most favorite gifts consisted of $8,000 automobiles and pianos valued from $1,200 to $3,500; she purchased eight grand pianos in one afternoon. Some of her other ostentatious presents included expensive cut glass, costly jewelry and tapestries, private chartered train trips to New York theater parties and fully paid European vacations. Her caretaker received an automobile, while cooks and maids wore sealskin coats. As wedding presents, Cassie presented a favorite clerk at one of downtown Cleveland's department stores a piano and a complete outfit of parlor furniture, rugs and carpets. Cassie didn't even know the clerk's name. A delivery boy from a butcher shop enjoyed her gift of a dozen handmade suits.

After spending much of her husband's savings, continuation of her lavish lifestyle required Cassie to develop novel swindling schemes much more extensive and creative than her past endeavors. Traveling to Pennsylvania, Cassie secured a loan by claiming an uncle had died, leaving a vast fortune that Andrew Carnegie had placed in trust for her uncle's imbecile son. By a provision of the will, Cassie would inherit the money when the imbecile died because the steel tycoon did not want the responsibility of administrating the trust. In another ploy, she claimed an uncle had died in New York, leaving her $7 million in stocks and bonds. But she needed a short-term loan of $30,000 to pay attorneys' fees before her lawyers would assist her in obtaining the money.

About this time, Cassie created her greatest scam by posing as the illegitimate daughter of Andrew Carnegie, an heiress whose father had promised her millions of dollars. The swindle began when Cassie traveled to New York with James Dillon, Dr. Chadwick's friend and attorney. Cassie's interest in Dillon involved neither his legal expertise nor his comradeship but, rather, his irresistible urge to spread gossip.

Dillon accompanied Cassie on a jaunt to the mansion of Andrew Carnegie. She entered the tycoon's home and, after a few minutes, returned with a large envelope containing securities allegedly valued at about $5 million along with two notes, both containing Carnegie's signature, one for $250,000 and the other for $500,000. She awkwardly and intentionally spilled the envelope's contents in sight of Dillon, to whom she then conveyed the amazing story of her secret father. Cassie claimed Carnegie provided the money "to right the wrong of my birth." Swearing Dillon to silence, she correctly anticipated he would spread the story as quickly as possible.

Cassie had actually entered the mansion by requesting references and information regarding a fictitious servant named Hilda Schmidt, who claimed to have been employed by the Carnegie family. The time required for Carnegie's staff to determine no record of the person existed matched perfectly the time Cassie needed to convince Dillon she had received the forged and worthless securities from Carnegie.

Cassie used the notes and securities, along with her Carnegie tale that had spread across the country, as collateral in securing loans from banks and private individuals. In Pittsburgh, she negotiated loans for $800,000 by using the fake securities and $3,000 in real jewelry she most likely smuggled into the United States from France. She artfully moved deposits, withdrawals, loan repayments and requests for new loans among various financial institutions, each time retaining a portion of the newly acquired money to support her extravagant lifestyle.

Ira Reynolds, the secretary-treasurer of Cleveland's Wade Park Bank and an old friend of Dr. Chadwick, turned into another of Cassie's victims. She borrowed more than $1 million, using a memorandum signed by Reynolds that claimed the bank possessed a package containing millions of dollars of her securities that included a $5 million note from Andrew Carnegie. Reynolds never even inspected the package.

Her extraordinary schemes collapsed in November 1904. Herbert B. Brown brought suit to recover the $190,000 he had loaned Cassie. Always

Cassie Chadwick received millions of dollars in loans by using as collateral a forged $5 million note supposedly signed by Andrew Carnegie. *Courtesy of Cleveland Public Library, Photograph Collection.*

in character, Cassie made it quite clear that she envisioned no problems: "There must be no misrepresentations. I expect to see everything adjusted within the course of the next few days." But Cleveland's queen of finance could not possibly pay back the debt.

Next, C.T. Beckwith, the president of Citizens National Bank in Oberlin, confessed he had made ill-advised loans to Cassie and even signed a note guaranteeing the forged signature of Andrew Carnegie. Incredibly, Beckwith had approved loans to Cassie amounting to about four times the worth of the bank, along with a loan of $102,000 using his own money. As the doors to the bank temporarily closed, Beckwith remained confident that Cassie would repay his debt, blaming her short-term dilemma on "unscrupulous men trying to cheat her out of money." He told reporters, "She is an honest woman and I know I will get my money back."

Unable to recover from its mammoth losses, the bank permanently closed, wiping out the life savings of many Oberlin residents. Beckwith changed his once optimistic outlook: "I am either an awful dupe or a terrible fool. I guess there is no doubt my being a fool." The uncanny similarity between Toledo's honest but deceived Joseph Lamb and Oberlin's highly respected but equally betrayed C.T. Beckwith raised suspicions that Cassie Chadwick and Madam DeVere might be the same person.

As Cassie's financial fantasies collapsed, Dr. Chadwick and the daughter from his first marriage disappeared in Europe. He purportedly fled the United States to recover from an illness and to supervise the education of his twenty-one-year-old daughter. When discovered in Paris, the doctor still rejected the evilness of his wife's intentions. In reporting Cassie's latest antics, Paris newspapers compared her to Theresa Humbert, a great 1880s French swindler who pretended to be an heir of Robert Crawford, a fictional American millionaire. Dr. Chadwick commented, "I noticed that the Paris newspapers are trying to draw an analogy between Mrs. Chadwick and Mme. Humbert. That is impossible. The Humbert woman deliberately defrauded people."

The once well-off Dr. Chadwick eventually divorced Cassie and declared bankruptcy to become free from any further obligations incurred by his former wife. At the time of his bankruptcy, his total assets amounted to $75, the value of his medical books and office fixtures. Dr. Chadwick relocated to New York, where he began a new practice. His daughter acquired a job in an uncle's Florida lumberyard office.

Cassie's known liabilities summed to about $1 million, but many of her victims (especially banks) chose not to press charges, which would publicize

BY THE KNICKERBOCKER ART GALLERIES OF NEW YORK

Now on Exhibition from 9 A. M. to 10 P. M.

AT THE URGENT REQUEST OF MANY CLEVELAND CITIZENS

The entire sumptuous Effects: Rugs, Paintings, Ivorys, and other Treasures of Art contained in the residence of

Mrs. Cassie L. Chadwick

1824 Euclid, cor. Genesee Ave.

Prior to absolute Sale.

In order to avoid overcrowding an admission of 50c will be charged.

A New York gallery placed Cassie Chadwick's art treasures on display in her Euclid Avenue home. *Courtesy of the* Plain Dealer.

Mrs. Chadwick

_Her personal property will be disposed of at

PRIVATE SALE

Mon., April 3

At GENERAL CARTAGE & STORAGE CO.'S SALES ROOMS

20 Viaduct

An auctioneer sold Cassie Chadwick's belongings to help pay her creditors. *Courtesy of the* Plain Dealer.

Convicted of fraud and sentenced to fourteen years in prison, Cassie's jail cell seemed quite austere compared with her previous Millionaires' Row environment. *Courtesy of Cleveland Public Library, Photograph Collection.*

their poor business instincts. Creditors eventually received about two cents on the dollar. Cassie remarked, "I even admit I did not borrow in a businesslike way. But you can't accuse a poor businesswoman of being a criminal, can you?" Following six days of testimony, Cassie's attorney adopted a somewhat analogous closing defense during her criminal trial: "A woman stands on one side and arrayed against her are all the forces of the great, the powerful, the magnificent United States government, the strongest, the mightiest and the most feared government in the world—and this tremendous crushing power stands as the accuser of this one weak woman."

The jury deliberated for five hours; its guilty verdict resulted in a ten-year prison sentence. During Cassie's prison confinement, an owner of a cow turned the Chadwicks' unkempt Euclid Avenue front lawn into a makeshift pasture, bringing his cow to graze in the morning and retrieving her in the evening. Cassie's health deteriorated rapidly following her incarceration. In 1907, after serving three years in prison, she died with virtually no possessions; an undertaker needed to purchase suitable clothing for her funeral.

At Cassie's interment, a newsreel cameraman ran out of film before her coffin had been completely lowered. After reloading the camera, he requested the coffin be raised and again lowered so he could obtain his prized photograph. A very irritated presiding minister accidentally bumped the cameraman into Cassie's open grave while his colleagues continued rolling their own cameras. Nickelodeon patrons throughout North America soon delighted in watching the humiliated cameraman climb out of Cassie Chadwick's grave.

Part IV

Business in the
Gilded Age

Chapter 11
An Attack of Brain Fever

O ne doctor attributed Horace Perry Weddell's bizarre actions to "an attack of brain fever," while another diagnosed him as "out of his mind." The *Cleveland Press* reported the Euclid Avenue millionaire had entered into "a wild delirium of mental excitement bordering on stark madness." The more conservative *Plain Dealer* described Weddell as being temporarily insane.

Not all of the mystifying events of the afternoon

A banker and railroad investor, Horace Weddell lived in a Euclid Avenue mansion for more than a half century. *Courtesy of Cleveland Public Library, Photograph Collection.*

and evening of November 10, 1884, are known with complete certainty since so few people actually witnessed the multiple dramas. What is generally agreed upon is that Horace, with a revolver in his hand, threatened to shoot his son Lawrence and his daughter, Mable. Retaining possession of the weapon after a struggle with Lawrence, Horace continued his rampage by attempting to kill the affluent Sylvester Thomas Everett, his business partner and Millionaires' Row neighbor. As Sylvester approached to within six feet of Weddell's stopped carriage, Horace jumped from the buggy, drew a pistol and shouted, "I've got you now." The

Sylvester Everett, a wealthy Euclid Avenue resident, succeeded as a banker, industrialist and political leader. *Courtesy of Cleveland Public Library, Photograph Collection.*

most accepted account is that Horace went so far as to point the gun at Sylvester's breast and pull the trigger; fortunately, the gun did not discharge.

Defending his life, Sylvester knocked Horace's arm and fought for control of the weapon. As the pair struggled, Horace muttered dire threats. Lawrence flagged down a passing streetcar whose conductor helped to disarm Horace. Sylvester raced into his home, returning with his own gun. Following the attempted murder, Sylvester told a *Cleveland Leader* reporter that he knew of no reason why Horace would want to take his life, commenting, "Mr. Weddell and I are the best of friends."

Although Horace's actions depicted an emotionally disturbed person, rational explanations for his strange deeds surfaced as additional information emerged. The tangled web included a business failure that threatened his entire fortune, a perceived swindle orchestrated by his partners, marital infidelity, a dying wife and a secret marriage.

Set back 250 feet from the street, Peter Weddell constructed his Euclid Avenue country home a few blocks past East Thirtieth Street. *Courtesy of Cleveland Public Library, Photograph Collection.*

Horace's father, Pennsylvania native Peter Martin Weddell, had owned one of Cleveland's first general stores. Peter met Sophia Perry, a daughter of Cleveland pioneer Nathan Perry Sr., in Newark, Ohio (in the Columbus metropolitan area), where she attended school. The two married, and in 1820, he founded his store on the corner of Superior Avenue and West Sixth Street.

As owner, salesman and bookkeeper of the store, Peter originally experienced little competition. He accumulated a fortune selling ladies' shoes ($1.62 a pair), twenty-one quills and a quire of writing paper ($1.50), calico ($0.03 per yard), molasses ($0.63 per gallon), flour ($4.00 per barrel), nails ($0.10 per pound), whiskey ($0.28 per gallon) and French brandy ($2.00 per gallon). Weddell also sold teas, coffees, rice, raisins, knives, forks, plates, handkerchiefs and roofing shingles.

In 1832, Peter built his Euclid Avenue residence on land with an eight-hundred-foot frontage, the widest on the street. The backyard extended a half mile to Payne Avenue. Peter used the home as a weekend sanctuary while still living on Superior Avenue during the hectic workweek. In 1847, he constructed the famous Weddell House hotel in downtown Cleveland visited by notable people from celebrity singer Jenny Lind to presidential candidate Abraham Lincoln. But Peter never witnessed the hotel's opening. On a business trip to New York to acquire furniture and decorations for the new hotel, he contracted typhoid fever and died. Prior to his death, Peter reigned as one of the richest men in Cleveland.

Born in Cleveland in 1823, Horace spent his first nine years growing up in his parents' combined residence and store. A banker and co-organizer of Ohio's first railroad, he inherited his parents' Euclid Avenue home, where he lived for fifty-two years before being forced out because of a scandal involving his neighbor Sylvester Everett.

Everett, born in 1838, spent his early youth laboring on his father's Ohio farm in Liberty Township. At the age of fourteen, he delivered messages for a Cleveland bank. Sixteen years later, he managed a banking house and later founded the National Bank of Commerce. Additionally, Sylvester pursued financial interests in iron ore companies, street railways, railroads and ranch properties and partnered with Mark Hanna in other business ventures and political activities.

After he served two terms as city treasurer, both the Republican and Democratic Parties supported Sylvester's reelection. Clevelanders eventually chose him as city treasurer a total of seven times, often without opposition. He actively promoted Republican Party issues at local, state and national levels. As a famous political leader, Clevelanders took pride in the city's homegrown luminary. But newspapers developed distrust for Everett and his growing political power, especially with Mark Hanna and other important political powerbrokers. The *Plain Dealer* called David A. Kimberly, the 1885 Republican candidate for city treasurer, "a puppet of a banking institution" nominated "by a ring for an improper purpose." The newspaper claimed Kimberly's nomination "was brought about by a combination made and controlled by Marcus A. Hanna and Sylvester T. Everett."

Horace's aggressive acts in 1884 are partly attributed to a business deal involving both Sylvester and his brother, Dr. Azariah Everett. Back in 1860, when the doctor embarked on organizing a private bank, he offered Horace an annual payment of $500 for the use of his name, although Horace would not share in the profits or management of the bank. Furthermore, Horace would be protected against any claims that might occur against the bank. The arrangement made good business sense since eastern bankers, a potential source of investment funds, knew and respected the Weddell name and reputation.

In 1883, the Everett brothers dissolved the bank, creating an organization with the same ownership arrangement. The new firm acquired the assets, liabilities and property of the former bank. Although Sylvester assured Horace that no problems would occur regarding the solvency of the new organization, he hurriedly sold his own interest in the bank. The bank failed within one year of its creation. Horace discovered he had no protection from claims against the new organization; the bank's failure wiped out most of his $1,200,000 fortune. The court issued an injunction preventing Horace from even visiting the Euclid Avenue mansion where he had lived.

Horace instituted a $1,200,000 lawsuit against the Everett brothers, the largest lawsuit ever initiated in Cuyahoga County up to that point. Dr. Everett told a reporter, "I can assure you that I have lost no sleep over the matter." In time, years of court battles settled all suits against the bank; the depositors received dollar-for-dollar payment with interest. The sale of Horace's Euclid Avenue home and a mortgage against the Weddell House hotel created part of the money used to pay depositors. An out-of-court settlement with Sylvester allowed Horace a measure of relief from his financial losses.

When Horace threatened Sylvester with murder, a family drama had been unfolding in Horace's life. He and his wife experienced marital problems severe enough for her to relocate to Europe with their three children (Lawrence, Mable and Frank), claiming their offspring would receive a more comprehensive education abroad. Eighteen years earlier, Mary Timmerman had entered the Weddell home as a nursemaid and continued as a housekeeper. Horace's prolonged affair with Mary had caused his wife's departure to Europe. The couple negotiated terms of a reconciliation that included Horace dismissing Mary as a household employee and constructing a new home for her. But Mrs. Weddell died in Europe prior to her reunion with Horace.

When the children arrived from Europe, Mary briefly moved to the home Horace had built for her. But turmoil erupted when the children stoutly objected to Mary's inevitable return to the household. Their callous attitude toward Mary created a very problematic situation for Horace, who had already secretly married Mary, the vows taken in Pennsylvania to avoid publicity. The couple apparently intended to keep the marriage a secret, but with Horace engaging in attempted murder, Mary divulged their marriage to ensure she held a valid claim to his estate.

The children recovered from the initial shock of learning about their new stepmother. Mable married and moved to New England. Lawrence and Frank developed into gentlemen worthy of Euclid Avenue society. On the evening of August 22, 1889, while waiting for their carriage on East Twelfth Street near Chester Avenue, the brothers became incensed at a "vile, horrible" name a group of street boys had called them. Lawrence struck one of the gang with the back of his walking stick. The boy returned with his mother, who slapped Lawrence in the face. A butcher boy witnessing the incident proceeded to deliver an even stronger blow to Lawrence, knocking off his top hat and causing him to drop the divisive walking stick. One of the boys ran off with the hat and stick, but police recovered both items while sympathizing with the brothers over their ordeal in being called such a despicable name. The street gang had referred to the Weddell brothers as "rich dudes."

Following the altercation with Horace, Sylvester encountered several serious business problems of his own. The directors of the First National Bank requested and received Sylvester's resignation because of his speculation in Northern Pacific Railroad stock. Although he had used his own money and in no way jeopardized the bank, the stock dealings violated the bank's ethics rules. In 1892, the East Cleveland Railroad charged Sylvester with illegally taking possession of fifteen of its $1,000 bonds and using the proceeds for personal purposes. Sylvester explained that he had acted legally because the railroad owed him money in excess of $15,000 as his commission for the sale of bonds. The railroad countered that Sylvester had no authority to sell the bonds and they never needed his services. Following claims, counterclaims, verdicts and appeals, four trials failed to establish a clear-cut winner in the dispute.

Despite these dilemmas, Sylvester continued as an influential political leader. President Garfield appointed him the government director of the Union Pacific Railroad, and President McKinley offered him an ambassadorship to Austria-Hungary. Although he had served as a delegate to Republican national conventions in 1872, 1880, 1888 and 1896, by 1900 Sylvester's political strength had weakened. He lost an election to represent northeast Ohio in the Republican convention that year and hinted that Mark Hanna, his former political colleague, had orchestrated his defeat. When a reporter asked Sylvester if the setback signaled his departure from politics, he responded, "Not by any means. I am only beginning." The crafty politician asked influential party members to select him as one of four Ohioans to be chosen as a delegate at large to the convention, but his effort failed.

Sylvester married in 1850; the union continued until his wife's death in 1876. Three years later, he wed the former Alice Louise Wade,

Opposite, top: Sylvester T. Everett's Romanesque Revival mansion, under construction in this photograph, dignified Euclid Avenue just east of the home of his wife's childhood residence. *Courtesy of Cleveland Public Library, Photograph Collection.*

Opposite, bottom: The Everett home encompassed three floors filled by thirty-five principal rooms, forty fireplaces, fifteen bedrooms and twelve bathrooms. *Courtesy of Cleveland Public Library, Photograph Collection.*

From this imposing balcony, Mrs. Everett welcomed presidents of the United States and other dignitaries. *Courtesy of Cleveland Public Library, Photograph Collection.*

granddaughter of Jeptha Homer Wade and only daughter of Randall P. Wade. The wedding took place in Randall's Euclid Avenue home. Grandfather Wade presented Sylvester with a check for $10,000; Alice received a diamond necklace, valued at $15,000 and containing forty-two choice stones and numerous smaller ones. Although the couple came from families representing some of Euclid Avenue's greatest wealth, their marriage did not appear to be one of convenience. The two thoroughly enjoyed each other's company on summer picnics, winter sleigh rides and theater and social events.

The Everett mansion, constructed in 1883 with four-foot-thick stone outer walls, featured a three-floor interior containing a total of thirty-five principal rooms along with twelve bathrooms and forty fireplaces. One room, completely soundproofed and intentionally designed without windows, served as an occasional refuge for Alice, who harbored an unusually intense fear of thunderstorms. Another room contained a carved wishing well and a star-shaped fountain shooting jets of water almost to the ceiling.

The Everett mansion's sixty-year-reign on Euclid Avenue personified the wealth and extravagance of Millionaires' Row. *Courtesy of Cleveland Public Library, Special Collections.*

Twenty-eight servants attended to the Everett mansion. Gold-leaf walls highlighted the master bedroom. The family decorated another bedroom with blue tiles and Scandinavian furnishings. Another of the home's fifteen bedrooms accentuated a Japanese motif. A Louis XVI drawing room focused on white mahogany, present even on the grand piano.

Jet-black ebony woodwork highlighted the appropriately named President's Room. At least five presidents (Harrison, Grant, Hayes, McKinley and Taft) visited the Everett mansion. Harding, also well acquainted with Everett, may also have been a guest at his home. Other notable visitors included financier J.P. Morgan, steel tycoon Andrew Carnegie, merchant John Wanamaker, banker Anthony Drexel, Civil War general Nelson A. Miles and Chinese statesman Li Hung Chang.

In addition to his Euclid Avenue home, Everett built a summer estate in North Carolina, about four miles from Vanderbilt's famous Biltmore mansion. As his interest in politics and business eventually waned, Everett also spent portions of the winter months in California.

In 1922, Everett died at the age of eighty-four in his extraordinary Euclid Avenue home. The family sold the mansion, which survived until 1938 as an apartment building with a small golf course embellishing the front lawn. In 1933, a visit by the Baroness Rudolph Oppenheim of Berlin and Harringsdorff, Germany, brought closure to the Everett family's connection to the once-great mansion. Paying her first visit to Cleveland in forty years, the baroness had grown up as Marguerite Everett, the daughter of Sylvester.

Despite the acute family feud, Lawrence Weddell married Eleanor Everett, another daughter of Sylvester. Tragically, in 1895, Lawrence died of pneumonia at the age of thirty-five. Horace Weddell, who lived to the age of ninety-one, died in 1914.

Chapter 12
Cleveland's Streetcar Wars

T om L. Johnson and Mark Hanna, two of Cleveland's richest
millionaires and biggest rivals, vigorously competed to control the
city's growing street rail (streetcar) systems. Their legendary, hard-hitting
business battles persisted for two decades. Johnson's social reforms as
Cleveland's mayor and Hanna's wealth suggest struggles between a
community activist and an affluent Victorian robber baron. Yet in the
first decade of their conflicts, two tough businessmen battled to determine
which one could generate the most profits.

Before the advent of electricity, horses pulled streetcars throughout the
city using rails embedded in the streets. By the mid-1880s, eight relatively
small, privately owned companies vied for city approval to expand their
routes, manage their fare structures and convert from horse to electric
power. Since coordination among the numerous streetcar lines did not
exist, riders often needed to use multiple companies to complete a single
trip, paying a new fare at transfer points among the systems. During this
chaotic period, Hanna inherited his father-in-law's streetcar businesses
and Johnson entered the Cleveland market. The combination set the stage
for the city's streetcar wars.

Born in 1854 into a wealthy Kentucky family owning about one hundred
slaves, Tom Loftin Johnson sold newspapers at the age of eleven to help support
his family, whose fortune in cotton vanished during the Civil War. At the age of
fifteen, Johnson counted fare money for a Louisville streetcar line. A few years
later, a relative lent him money to purchase a failing Indianapolis streetcar

system powered by mules. Johnson reorganized the declining company, turning it into a highly profitable business. He invented a more efficient trolley fare box and used the licensing royalties to invest in street railroads and steel companies throughout the United States. His steel mills produced the rails needed to manufacture the streetcar tracks.

Temporarily relocating to Cleveland in 1883, Johnson purchased and lavishly remodeled the former Euclid Avenue residence of millionaire George Stockley, who had moved to New York. He even added an enclosed ice-skating rink in the backyard. At Johnson's insistence, workmen applied

Once a millionaire capitalist and then a progressive mayor, Tom L. Johnson has remained a controversial character in Cleveland's history. *Courtesy of Cleveland Public Library, Photograph Collection.*

coats of grease and dust to the new annex, matching the appearance of the existing home. When a worker asked Johnson why he didn't clean the house instead, the millionaire replied, "Any fool could have done that." Notwithstanding his ownership of a Euclid Avenue mansion, Johnson initially spent little time in the city.

Marcus Alonzo Hanna, born in 1837 in Lisbon, Ohio, moved to Cleveland with his family as a teen. He briefly attended Western Reserve College (then located in Hudson, Ohio), but the school expelled him when he handed out fake satirical programs at a somber ceremonial affair. Hanna then served in various capacities in the family's wholesale grocery business and commission house located in the Flats.

In 1862, Hanna met Charlotte Augusta Rhodes shortly after her return to Cleveland following her education at a fancy finishing school. Her father, the ardent Democrat Daniel Rhodes, in time almost grudgingly granted the equally passionate Republican Hanna permission to marry his daughter.

Above: Tom L. Johnson resided in this Millionaires' Row mansion. *Courtesy of Cleveland Public Library, Photograph Collection.*

Left: Mark Hanna combined wealth and political power to become one of Cleveland's most powerful millionaires. *Courtesy of Cleveland Public Library, Photograph Collection.*

Using business instincts that needed significant fine-tuning, Hanna spent his limited savings to construct an oil refinery and invest in a Great Lakes steamer. The refinery burned to the ground, and the ship sank into a lake; the two misfortunes wiped out Hanna's savings.

Rhodes hired the failed entrepreneur and retired shortly afterward. The firm Rhodes and Company (later M.A. Hanna and Company) dealt principally in coal, iron and steel but under Hanna's control expanded into other fields, including the building of ships to carry the company's freight. The firm also maintained close relationships with railroads, another source of transportation. Hanna also served as director of two railroads.

The first skirmish between Johnson and Hanna took place in 1879, even before Johnson had moved to Cleveland. Street rail companies required route franchises granted by city council. Political connections and illegal payoffs seemed to play an important role in obtaining these permits. Johnson bid on a franchise owned by Hanna but up for review and renewal. Although Johnson presented a more cost-effective bid, Cleveland city council members remained loyal to Hanna.

Undaunted by his defeat, Johnson successfully entered the Cleveland market by purchasing a streetcar company whose only asset consisted of a short route on West Twenty-fifth Street. The line started near Riverside Cemetery and terminated just before it reached a Lorain Road market near the current West Side Market. The company's antiquated infrastructure consisted of tracks described as "two streaks of rust" along with one ancient car and two elderly mules. But with his experience in transforming the old Indianapolis company, Johnson already possessed the expertise to modernize the West Twenty-fifth Street line.

The Superior Viaduct, leading directly into downtown Cleveland, sat just a half mile to the north of Johnson's streetcar route. But Hanna, a major stockholder in the railroad connecting West Twenty-fifth Street to the viaduct, prevented Johnson from providing direct service from the west side into downtown. Johnson adeptly turned Hanna's refusal to share the tracks into a political issue. Yet boisterous city council meetings, extending into the early morning hours, failed to reach any resolution.

Exerting very levelheaded patience, Johnson won the skirmish's second round. At the next renewal hearing, the city refused to continue Hanna's franchise unless he allowed Johnson to share the tracks. In addition to his business triumph, Johnson demonstrated that a virtual outsider to Cleveland could successfully upstage Hanna, a political powerhouse at the national level. Johnson purchased another local railway company and then defeated

This streetcar traveled down West Twenty-fifth Street in 1890, about the time Johnson and Hanna battled for control of the street's streetcar franchise. *Courtesy of Cleveland Public Library, Photograph Collection.*

Hanna in obtaining an important east side line, enabling him to connect Cleveland's east and west sides with downtown for a single fare.

The hostilities continued throughout the 1880s. In 1889, the *Plain Dealer* reported that the Cleveland Board of Improvements listened to "rather hot words between Hanna and Johnson" regarding a new track to be laid on Superior Avenue between Public Square and the Central Viaduct. Initially, Johnson received the permit, but the city subsequently revoked it "to allow more time for discussion." Johnson threatened to start work anyway, claiming that "nothing but the police or an injunction" would stop him. The city responded by issuing the injunction.

During this period, Johnson had studied *Social Problems* and *Progress and Poverty*, two books written by the influential political thinker Henry George. In George's judgment, poverty, inequality and unemployment resulted directly from increases in land values and would be eliminated through purging all taxes except for a single tax on land. Although Johnson did not become an immediate convert, he met with George, who resided in New York, to discuss his ideas. In time, the two developed a close friendship and political alliance.

In 1888, Johnson turned to politics but suffered a decisive defeat running for a seat in the House of Representatives. He returned to win two consecutive terms before being defeated again in 1894. In that year, Johnson aroused the wrath of Clevelanders in a political blunder in which he asserted that the city's dedicated Democrat Henry Payne acted like a protectionist and, therefore, by default, a Republican. The *Plain Dealer* lashed out at Johnson, labeling him "a carpetbagger from Kentucky who came to Cleveland, not to make it greater, but to put money in his own pocket." After his political defeat, he returned to manage his lucrative street railway business. Outwardly, Johnson continued to display the characteristics of a rich capitalist, although his views on capitalism and government would soon change significantly.

In 1895, Johnson and rival Henry A. Everett (who had developed the world's first successful electrified street rail) clashed over the cost of streetcar fares. Everett, the son of Dr. Azariah Everett and nephew of Euclid Avenue's Sylvester Everett, sought to establish a franchise to build three-cent-ride streetcar lines, while Johnson, still the entrepreneur, promoted a higher five-cent fare. Everett characterized Johnson to a *Plain Dealer* reporter in these words: "Tom Johnson is a double-dyed hypocrite. He never did anything for anyone unless he expected to get it back tenfold." Claiming few riders actually traveled the railway's entire distance in a single ride, Everett continued, "I can imagine my fat friend with tears in his eyes saying: 'Think of it! We carry a passenger 13 miles for five cents.' As a matter of actual figuring, the street railways only carry one passenger out of every 10,000 over the entire 13 miles. To pay for this one man, they level tribute on the other 9,999." He concluded his interview with this suggestion: "I advise the people of Cleveland to organize and force the companies to give them a three-cent fare."

By 1899, Johnson's assets had reached $2,500,000, although he reportedly owed Cuyahoga County $433,383.90 in back taxes on stocks, bonds and personal property that he had failed to report. At this point, the streetcar wars took a markedly unexpected turn. Johnson convinced himself he could no longer own and profit from street railroads while simultaneously expounding on the visions of Henry George. This realization prompted him to sell all his interests in streetcar companies and manufacturing businesses.

In 1901, Johnson entered the Cleveland mayoral race, using tents and the ice-skating facility in his Euclid Avenue mansion as forums for political gatherings. As a politician, he saw no contradiction in his platform to municipalize the streetcar lines that, as private businesses, had created

Tom L. Johnson and his sons Loftin and Arthur (back) posed in Johnson's Winton automobile, which he used in 1903 to travel throughout the state campaigning for governor. His mansion is in the background (left). *Courtesy of Cleveland Public Library, Photograph Collection.*

his own fortune. Johnson reasoned that a smart businessman (such as himself) would take advantage of any opportunities given to him. The citizens of Cleveland should therefore concentrate on reducing business perks rather than dwelling on his own past history. In campaigning against the evils of streetcar barons, he spoke with great authority since he had been one of the evilest. But now he advocated the three-cent fare that he had previously opposed.

Johnson won the election, gaining 54 percent of the vote. But the animosity between the mayor and Hanna continued unabated. In 1903, as keynote speaker to begin the Ohio Republican campaigns, Hanna (now a state senator) provided this assessment of Johnson and his supporters: "A carpetbagger followed by a train of all the howling political vagrants of Ohio, with a crazy quilt ticket and pretending to stand upon a pessimistic, socialistic and anarchistic platform." Johnson easily won his second term in office, furthering diminishing Hanna's power and prestige.

The 260-pound Tom L. Johnson campaigned for reelection in 1905.
Courtesy of Cleveland Public Library, Photograph Collection.

The battle between Johnson and Hanna ended when the senator died in 1904. Members of the presidential cabinet, financier J.P. Morgan, local and state politicians and many other friends attended Hanna's funeral at St. Paul's Episcopal Church located on Millionaires' Row at Euclid Avenue and East Fortieth Street. Johnson, Hanna's old nemesis, requested all business stop in the city for five minutes to offer "a fitting expression of the public sense of loss in the death of our distinguished citizen, the Honorable M.A. Hanna, senator of the United States from the state of Ohio." Businesses and citizens in Cleveland and across the state observed Johnson's request. But Johnson's streetcar conflicts continued with other powerful streetcar owners.

Johnson finally organized the city-owned Municipal Traction Company, which inherited Johnson's old Forest City railway. The new streetcar organization immediately implemented a three-cent fare and easily overwhelmed competition from the remaining privately owned five-cent fare companies. But streetcar expert Peter Witt, using a colorful analogy, advised Johnson to totally annihilate the private businesses: "The snake will not be dead unless you crush its head. As long as there is life in it, it will coil itself around our legs and you won't even be able to walk. Kill the damned beast." Witt's advice proved to be very prophetic as the mayor's splendid three-cent fare dream turned into an abysmal nightmare.

Workers expected the Municipal Traction Company to honor the contracts of the old private companies and walked off their jobs when they did not receive expected raises. Johnson, the champion of the working man, allowed

On November 1, 1906, the Municipal Traction Company initiated its first three-cent fare rides. Beginning on Denison Avenue, the route terminated at West Twenty-eighth Street and Detroit Avenue, the location of this image. *Courtesy of Cleveland Public Library, Photograph Collection.*

the new municipal-owned firm to hire strikebreakers. Violence erupted quickly as strikers hurled stones at passengers and crewmen and placed boulders, trees and dynamite on the tracks. The aggression culminated in gunfire.

In Johnson's election campaigns, the very experienced streetcar owner promised voters he possessed the expertise to implement a three-cent fare without cutting any service; in fact, Johnson guaranteed even better service. After implementing his municipal company, Johnson directly contradicted his pledges to Clevelanders by eliminating many long-established but unprofitable routes and drastically cutting service times on other lines. Streetcars arrived late and sometimes not at all; cars stopped at wrong corners, causing customers to miss their rides. The new company charged students and poor people for transportation to Euclid Beach amusement park while the previous private company had offered free rides as a public service gesture.

At the same time that the mayor reneged on his promises, the State of Ohio passed a referendum law (endorsed by Johnson) in conjunction with street railway franchises. The leaders of Cleveland's suffering private streetcar companies acquired enough signatures of disgruntled customers to force an election to approve or reject Johnson's new municipal company. The mayor, apparently an ardent advocate of referendums unless they applied to him, unsuccessfully attempted to invalidate the petition signatures, spoke against the referendum and stalled the vote through court maneuvers.

When the voting day finally arrived, Clevelanders ended the municipal streetcar company's existence. A court declared the company bankrupt and discovered Johnson had used $35,000 of the railway's funds to form a private business to manufacture fare boxes. A new company kept the three-cent fare on some high-volume lines but increased the price on others to six tickets for a quarter and added a one-cent transfer charge among routes. In 1909, Johnson lost his bid for a fifth term as mayor, partly because of the streetcar fiasco and also because of his failing health caused by cirrhosis of the liver.

Despite his colossal failure, Johnson accomplished many very notable achievements. Today he seems to be especially revered for removing the "Keep off the Grass" signs from public places. Yet during his four terms as mayor, Johnson's administration also promoted and implemented the paving of miles of streets, advocated new milk and meat inspections standards, converted vacant lots into playgrounds and expanded the park system.

Johnson, who entered the mayor's office as a rich and vigorous man, exited with few assets and a disease-ridden body. His wealth declined as he paid sizeable debts incurred by his deceased brother while he could no

WILL ERECT BUILDING
132 FT. FRONTAGE
SPACE ARRANGED SUIT TENANT
THE
GREENLUND KENNERDELL
COMPANY.
WILLIAMSON BLDG.

Following Johnson's financial failures, his former mansion sat vacant, ready for demolition. *Courtesy of Cleveland Public Library, Photograph Collection.*

longer rely on dividends and stock price increases created by his former business holdings. He invested in the stock of his beloved Municipal Traction Company and lost the entire investment with the company's bankruptcy. He also never adjusted his lifestyle to match that of a mayor. In 1908, Johnson stated publicly that his fortune had disappeared. Meanwhile, his liver ailment steadily worsened.

Johnson sold his Millionaires' Row mansion, moving to the Knickerbocker Apartments on Euclid Avenue and then to the Whitehall Hotel in University Circle. The day before he died, the former mayor composed a letter to Napoleon Lajoie, manager of the Cleveland Naps baseball club, urging the team to fight for the pennant that year. As Johnson lay on his deathbed in 1911 at the age of fifty-six, William Jennings Bryan paid him a farewell visit. Johnson chose to be buried near Henry George in Brooklyn's Greenwood Cemetery. Millionaires, politicians, streetcar conductors and followers of both George and Johnson all attended the burial service.

New owners of Johnson's former mansion briefly operated it as an apartment house. A real estate company targeted buyers interested in razing the home and constructing a new building. In 1926, Ohio Motors finally purchased the mansion and surrounding land to build a showroom and office building. Johnson's former front lawn formed the nucleus of a used car lot that persisted for four decades. In the 1950s, a *Cleveland News* reader claimed he had obtained a piece of mahogany from a pilaster in the home. A guitar maker used the wood to construct the neck for a guitar that the reader still played. A 1969 Cleveland State University science building ended the site's run as a used car lot.

Chapter 13
Violence in the Mills

A rmed with a pistol in his pocket, striking union worker Sydney Davis threatened to shoot a man attempting to return to work at the Cleveland Rolling Mill. On the opposite side of the bitter 1882 labor dispute, police arrested non-union laborer Thomas Blythe as he entered the mill carrying a loaded revolver. On his next trip to work, a crowd attacked Blythe, crushing his skull, beating his nose "into jelly" and kicking him so violently that a displaced rib injured an internal organ. Originally listed in critical condition and not expected to live, Blythe recovered from the

Henry Chisholm, once a poor immigrant from Scotland, acquired his fortune in Cleveland. *Courtesy of Special Collections, Michael Schwartz Library, Cleveland State University.*

brutal attack. The violence broke out shortly after the death of Euclid Avenue millionaire Henry Chisholm, the mill's co-founder and president.

Born in 1822 in Scotland, Henry Chisholm dropped out of school at the age of twelve, entering the workforce as a carpenter's apprentice to support his widowed mother. When his apprenticeship ended, Chisholm relocated to Glasgow, where he labored as a journeyman carpenter. In 1842, the almost penniless Chisholm immigrated to Montreal to toil as a contract carpenter.

In 1850, Chisholm constructed a break wall (breakwater) at a Cleveland lakefront train terminal and remained in the city to build docks and

Henry Chisholm's Tuscan villa mansion is the first home to the left in this 1865 photograph of Euclid Avenue's north side looking east toward East Ninth Street. *Courtesy of Cleveland Public Library, Photograph Collection.*

piers. Meanwhile, brothers David and John Jones, entrepreneurs from Pennsylvania, constructed a steel mill to reroll worn-out iron rails. The two founders, requiring additional investors, added partners Andros B. Stone (the brother of millionaire Amasa Stone) and Henry Chisholm, who invested his life savings of $25,000. By 1858, the renamed Stone, Chisholm & Jones Company produced fifty tons of rerolled rails daily. Chisholm directed the firm's finances and employees, offering company-owned housing and company store benefits to the approximately 125 workers, each of whom knew Chisholm personally.

In 1863, Chisholm and Stone joined three other Euclid Avenue millionaires (Stillman Witt, Jeptha H. Wade and Henry B. Payne) to incorporate the Cleveland Rolling Mill Company, which absorbed the existing company. Through Chisholm's encouragement and research, the new business in 1865 constructed America's second Bessemer steel works, a process that dramatically lowered costs while reducing labor requirements. Chisholm also served as a director of the city's three leading banks.

Following the 1881 death of Henry Chisholm, and the succession of his son William to the presidency of the mill, employees issued a statement declaring they "feel assured that, under the new management, the feeling of goodwill will still continue as in the past." Yet Henry's commendable people skills seemed completely absent in his son. Under William's leadership, the mill would soon be engulfed in a pair of fiery labor strikes. But the bitter labor unrest actually began under Henry's command.

In 1874, a work stoppage had occurred when the company cut the pay of blast furnace employees by 10 percent (from $2.00 to $1.80 per hour) because of a business downturn and reduced demand for iron due to a

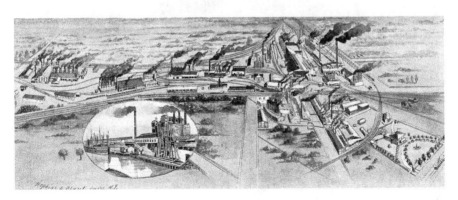

The Cleveland Rolling Mill, located on the southeast side of the city, witnessed several violent labor strikes. *Courtesy of Cleveland Public Library, Photograph Collection.*

decline in railroad building. When the employees refused to work for the lowered pay, management held back their already-earned wages, citing a clause in their contract requiring a three-week notice prior to leaving the job.

Three years later, following another reduction in wages, the mill's employees responded with a derisive letter to management: "We were perfectly astounded at your magnanimity of soul, but excuse us, gentlemen, we had forgotten that corporations have no souls, and we are beginning to doubt very much whether they have a conscience." The letter concluded, "The proposition is a direct insult to the feelings and intelligence of the men and one which they will not submit to."

Henry Chisholm, the president of the mill during both labor conflicts, somehow escaped the wrath of the millworkers. In fact, when he died, the employees contributed generously toward construction of a monument to commemorate their leader.

With William Chisholm now at the company's helm and economic instability continuing, labor strife erupted again on May 10, 1882, when five thousand employees ceased work to protest a reduction in wages, unsuitable working conditions and the failure of the company to recognize

William Chisholm (Henry's son) resided in this Euclid Avenue home, constructed in 1895, until his death in 1905. *Courtesy of Cleveland Public Library, Photograph Collection.*

labor unions. The company responded by posting a notice announcing the immediate hiring of non-union replacement workers.

By the 1880s, many former small, family-owned businesses had developed into much larger companies. Yet the founding families often viewed the businesses as their property because they had invested their own money, time and intelligence in making the companies successful. Interviews with William Chisholm and Henry B. Payne, appearing in the *Plain Dealer* at the time of the 1882 strike, clearly reflect that attitude. Chisholm explained:

> *Until within a few months ago, the employees of our company had not been connected with the labor organization known as the Iron and Steel Workers' Association. Lately however, they have been gathered into this organization and the result has been discontent and trouble to the company. The question was not a matter of wages so much as whether the Amalgamated Association should control our affairs and dictate to us our method of doing business.*

Payne added, "Two-thirds of the old employees would return to work immediately if they dared. Had it not been for meddlesome outsiders, the men would never have thought of striking the company." A staunch Democrat throughout his life, Payne also noted, "If the proprietors cannot discharge a man, no matter how useless, without permission from a union, if it cannot regulate its affairs in its own way, it might just as well go out of business."

Born in Hamilton, New York, Payne relocated to Cleveland in 1833 to study law with Hiram V. Willson, his future partner. Their firm prospered as clients bought and sold property in the flourishing city. Payne married Mary Perry, the richest female in town and the only daughter of his Euclid Avenue neighbor Nathan Perry Jr. Payne became the first Clevelander to be elected to the U.S. Senate and also served in the U.S. House of Representatives.

Only two years prior to the 1882 strike, Payne participated in the first of two earnest campaigns to become president of the United States. At a national level, discussion regarding Payne as a presidential candidate began in 1878 when the *Boston Globe* editorialized, "Give us the old Henry of the west." Although receiving eighty votes on the first ballot, Payne lost his 1880 presidential bid when the Democratic Party chose General Winfield Scott Hancock to run against James Garfield, another candidate with strong northeast Ohio ties. As Payne planned for the 1884 presidential nomination, momentum mounted for him to run for Ohio governor. Winning the contest in January 1884, his presidential aspirations faded enough for the party to select Grover Cleveland as its nominee.

As an attorney, politician and railroad executive, Payne welcomed many important visitors to his Millionaires' Row home. Civil War general Phil Sheridan (a frequent house guest) enjoyed croquet matches on Payne's front lawn. Presidential candidate Stephen A. Douglas, running against Abraham Lincoln, sought Payne's hospitality and political advice.

During the 1882 strike, Chisholm, Payne and other major stockholders reopened the mill using unskilled Polish and Czech recruits. A week later, striking workers attacked and hurled rocks at police and the hated strikebreakers. The company had armed replacement workers with revolvers; the striking employees and temporary strikebreakers exchanged gunfire at the end of a work shift. The beating of Thomas Blythe soon followed. After a group of unruly men entered the boardinghouse where replacement worker Henry Schulz resided, he escaped through a window and asked police to lock him up "for safekeeping." Newspapers and much of the public supported the company, while the union failed to meaningfully intimidate the strikebreakers. By the end of July, the strike had collapsed.

Just two years later, the company again agitated employees by implementing a ten percent reduction in pay. The indignant workers seemed to become even more aroused when the mill's executives banned workers from frequenting saloons during working hours, including lunch and dinner breaks.

A more massive and violent strike erupted in the summer of 1885 as workers protested wage cuts in response to another business recession. Five hundred workers marched to Chisholm's downtown office to demand a restoration of their wages. When Chisholm refused, a group of one thousand workers closed two other companies in which Chisholm owned substantial stock and invaded Chisholm-owned mills not even involved in the labor dispute.

The strikers' tactics did not generate sympathy from the newspapers. The *Plain Dealer* editorialized, "The woods seem to be full of anarchists and agitators who seem to think that the present labor troubles form an excellent opportunity for the sowing of the seeds of their pernicious doctrines."

After the union conducted a meeting in a vacant field on Fullerton Avenue, about one thousand strikers headed for the mill, where they met two solid lines of policemen. The strikers showered the lawmen with stones, many hitting their intended targets, and then rushed the police. The officers, outnumbered by about ten to one, stopped the strikers by using clubs but did not fire a shot. The strikers dispersed, many running away to avoid arrest. Meanwhile, a watchman at one of the gates, not directly involved in the conflict, died of a heart attack.

The next day, about two thousand strikers gathered in a vacant lot on Hamm Avenue just off Broadway Avenue. Speakers delivering speeches in English, Polish, Bohemian and German talked passionately about seeking revenge against the police, the Chisholm family and the mayor; fortunately, no violence occurred. The company, citing the dangers associated with workers attempting to do their job, closed the entire mill "until such time as the employees decide to return peaceably to work."

As the strike persisted into its third month, a crowd of more than one hundred Poles and Bohemians assailed foreman Wallace Kenerson as he drove to work. He drew his revolver and ordered the crowd to stand back. As the crowd drew closer, Kenerson fired into the crowd three times, hitting a striker on the arm. The incident ended when police arrived.

Nearby businesses struggled financially as the work stoppage continued. Grocers and butchers, suffering from decreased sales and unpaid credit accounts, contemplated bankruptcy. Many employees promised to return to their jobs but only if protected by police. The wives of workers who indicated a willingness to cross picket lines received threats claiming their houses would be burned down. The landlord of one of these employees told police that he would "suffer bad consequences" unless he evicted the tenant. At least one worker endured a physical attack on Broadway Avenue after finishing his shift.

The three-month strike ended when Cleveland mayor George Gardner ordered Chisholm to restore the June wage cut, thus eliminating the cause of the strike. But Chisholm refused to rehire many of his former workers, especially the leaders of the labor unrest.

William eventually sold the company and retired to concentrate on his golf game and annual European cruises. He lived in his Euclid Avenue mansion (constructed in 1895) until 1905, when he died from a stroke while purchasing a new coat in a Prospect Avenue tailor shop.

In 1911, Dr. William Thomas Corlett, a distinguished dermatologist, purchased William Chisholm's residence, adding a large annex to the west for use as an office. In the 1920s, Corlett rented the home to the Elks' Club when he moved to East Boulevard. The legendary Canadian orchestra leader Guy Lombardo made his first U.S. appearance at that venue. From the 1940s into the early 1960s, the old Chisholm home served as a rooming house. In 1965, Holiday Inn constructed a still-existing ten-story hotel on the site. The décor of the hotel's restaurant incorporated chandeliers, stained-glass windows and oak doors salvaged from the former home.

The Cleveland Rolling Mill eventually became incorporated into U.S. Steel.

Chapter 14
Ida Tarbell

The Rockefeller Nemesis

B eginning with his very first paycheck as a struggling teenager, John D. Rockefeller contributed 10 percent of his earnings to his church. He continued this practice throughout his life, even before charitable contributions had developed into a sophisticated component of income tax and estate planning. As Rockefeller grew wealthy, he supported his church not only financially but also by dedicating his valuable time, especially in the church's Sunday school activities. In 1864, Rockefeller married Laura Celestia Spelman, his high school sweetheart. The couple remained married, without a hint of scandal, for more than a half century until her death in 1915. He lived another twenty-two years but never remarried.

Despite his admirable personal life, Rockefeller's business practices created controversy for decades. Accurate and plentiful documentation suggests that Rockefeller first offered fair terms to buy out his often floundering competitors. Those choosing Standard Oil stock as payment reaped incredible wealth far above what their companies could have achieved alone. Stephen Harkness, a silent co-founder of Standard Oil, witnessed his $75,000 investment soar to more than $300 million. But small refiners who chose to remain independent of Standard Oil rarely succeeded. Rockefeller supposedly threatened competitors who refused his offers with bankruptcy, after which he would repurchase their assets at a lower cost. Rockefeller's combination of success and intimidation proved to be very effective. In a six-week period in 1872, he purchased twenty-two of his twenty-six Cleveland competitors and then invaded

John D. Rockefeller
rose from a modest
upbringing to
become the richest
man in the world.
*Courtesy of Cleveland
Public Library,
Photograph Collection.*

Pittsburgh, Philadelphia, Baltimore, New York and other refining centers to consolidate their operations as well.

In many cases, Rockefeller did not require underhanded tactics to eliminate his rivals; poor business practices created their own undoing. In one instance, owners of a Cleveland firm agreed to a standard covenant not to compete when they sold their business to Rockefeller. Within a short time, they initiated a new oil refining operation clearly in violation of their contract. Rather than pursuing a legal remedy, Rockefeller established an agreement whereby the owners agreed to limit the company's production in exchange for a guaranteed profit. When the company exceeded its production quota, Rockefeller sued, lost and disassociated himself from the company's business. Without Rockefeller's guidance and power, the firm soon failed.

A key component in expanding Rockefeller's refining empire involved minimization of rail transportation charges. The oil baron experienced little

A partnership between John D. Rockefeller and Stephen Harkness created almost unbelievable wealth for Harkness, allowing him to construct this stately Italianate villa on Euclid Avenue. *Courtesy of Cleveland Public Library, Photograph Collection.*

difficulty conversing with railroad executives; his Euclid Avenue neighbor Amasa Stone reigned as president of the powerful New York Central line, while John Henry Devereux, another Millionaires' Row resident, served as a vice-president.

The South Improvement Company provides a vivid illustration of the convoluted tactics used by Rockefeller and other large oil refiners in conjunction with the railroads. Created in 1871 by the president of the Pennsylvania Railroad, South Improvement sought to persuade other railroads to increase their rates by as much as 100 percent. South Improvement would then reimburse the few large refiners by paying them enormous rebates on their shipments. The refiners also shared part of the excessive rates charged to their smaller competitors. In return, the refiners would commit to a steady stream of business for the railroads. Thus, not only would smaller companies incur much higher shipping costs, but they

Early unsophisticated refineries (such as Rockefeller's Cleveland business in 1870) required minimal construction cost while satisfying increasing customer demand. *Courtesy of Special Collections, Michael Schwartz Library, Cleveland State University.*

would also contribute to the profits of the larger refiners that attempted to put them out of business. To further reduce competition, the railroads would provide participating refiners with reports delineating the smaller companies' shipping destinations, costs and dates.

Under this projected arrangement, the posted cost for shipping oil from Cleveland to New York would almost double to $2.56 per barrel. The railroad would pay the South Improvement Company a $1.06 fee per barrel, justified as compensation for South Improvement providing tank cars and loading facilities. The remaining revenues of the South Improvement would ultimately be divided among the railroads and the largest oil refiners.

As newspapers leaked details of this proposed business, outraged independent oil refiners and the public became more aware of the intimidating methods and cutthroat operations used to eliminate small competitors. The Pennsylvania legislature repealed the South Improvement

By 1889, Rockefeller's Cleveland refinery acted as the early flagship operation for the Standard Oil's growing empire. *Courtesy of Cleveland Public Library, Photograph Collection.*

Company's charter before the dubious company could conduct its first transaction. Most businesses incorrectly viewed Rockefeller as the architect of the conspiracy. Yet although competitors disliked Standard Oil, consumers never seemed to complain about the lower prices passed on through the company's brutally resourceful business practices.

By the end of the 1870s, Standard Oil refined more than 90 percent of the oil in the United States. In 1883, the *New York Sun* published an article profiling Cleveland's millionaires. Describing John D. Rockefeller, the newspaper noted, "He takes no part in politics, asks advice of no one and is his own master in all things." As the 1880s ended, well-informed business associates estimated Rockefeller's annual income had reached $9 million.

As the daughter of a modest oil refiner, Ida Minerva Tarbell acquired firsthand experience into why smaller businesses failed while Rockefeller enhanced his fortune. Born in a log cabin in 1857, Tarbell grew up witnessing the oil boom in northwestern Pennsylvania; she even lived for a time in Titusville, where the commercial oil drilling industry began. Her father had constructed wooden

Above: John D. Rockefeller's home, near the intersection of Euclid Avenue and East Fortieth Street, lacked the fancy arches, pitched roof, dormers, turrets and towers commonly incorporated in his neighbors' more extravagant homes. *Courtesy of Cleveland Public Library, Photograph Collection.*

Left: Ida Tarbell gained fame as a muckraker journalist. Her greatest success involved exposés of John Rockefeller's Standard Oil Company. *Courtesy of Cleveland Public Library, Photograph Collection.*

storage tanks for the transportation of oil and later became a small oil producer and refiner. Tarbell later accused Standard Oil of using unfair tactics to ruin her father's business, along with those of many other small oil refiners.

After graduating from Allegheny College, Tarbell taught high school science courses but resigned after two years. Gravitating toward a career in writing, she began in New York by composing material for a teaching supplement used with home study courses. In 1890, she relocated to Paris to conduct research for a biography of Madame Roland, the leader of an influential salon during the French Revolution. While in France, she wrote articles for various magazines. Her work came to the attention of magazine publisher Samuel McClure, who offered her a job. While working for *McClure's Magazine*, Tarbell developed a national reputation by composing multiple-part series profiling Napoleon Bonaparte and Abraham Lincoln.

In 1900, Tarbell started research on her next subject, the history of the Standard Oil Company. Although hardly unbiased, she painstakingly examined volumes of public records including lawsuit documentations, court testimony, state and federal reports, church records and newspaper articles. She even visited Rockefeller's church in Cleveland and observed him at one of the services. Tarbell amplified her findings through interviews with the Standard Oil executives, competitors, government regulators and academic experts (although she apparently never requested an interview with Rockefeller).

Tarbell's exposé of Standard Oil began in the November 1902 issue of *McClure's* and continued for a total of nineteen installments. She presented a wide-ranging portrayal of Standard Oil's unethical tactics while depicting small refiners, such as her father, as victims of Rockefeller's greed. She documented her interpretation of the company's unscrupulous espionage schemes, devastating price wars and intimidating marketing strategies. Tarbell added a two-part character study of Rockefeller, then in his mid-sixties. She portrayed him as looking like "the oldest man in the world, a living mummy." She depicted the millionaire as both money-grabbing and brutally effective. But Tarbell also mentioned Rockefeller's other side—the family man, churchgoer and supporter of charities. She viewed the oil king as two different people, one a warm human being representing virtue and the other a ruthless businessman symbolizing evil.

After publication of the Tarbell exposé, Cleveland's community leaders organized a visit to Rockefeller's Forrest Hill estate in East Cleveland to show their support for the millionaire. He personally greeted every one of the approximately four hundred guests.

John D. Rockefeller is pictured in 1911, about the time the Supreme Court found Standard Oil guilty of antitrust abuse. *Courtesy of Special Collections, Michael Schwartz Library, Cleveland State University.*

In 1911, the Supreme Court found Standard Oil guilty of antitrust violations and ordered the divesture of the company from its subsidiaries, thus ending the life of the great oil trust. But the thirty-three smaller companies (operating as Sohio, Exxon, Mobil, Chevron, Amoco, Esso and others) still dominated the oil market for decades.

For many years, Rockefeller never responded to Tarbell's writings, nor did he mention her name in public. Even when he finally discussed Tarbell, he carefully avoided controversy, instead only insisting he made his fortune honestly and honorably. He died of arteriosclerosis on May 23, 1937, less than two months shy of his ninety-eighth birthday.

Tarbell continued the "investigative reporting" format she helped initiate by composing articles concerning women's issues, labor and management relations, the politics of tariffs and less scathing biographies of Elbert Gary (U.S. Steel) and Owen D. Young (General Electric), along with her autobiography. In 1944, she died of pneumonia at the age of eighty-six.

Chapter 15
The Incredible Electricity Rivalries

E ven before attending Cleveland's Central High School, Charles Brush had developed a passionate interest in mechanical devices. He constructed makeshift microscopes and telescopes, creating every part of the instruments himself; Brush even ground his own lenses. As a high school student, he invented a device that used electricity to turn gas street lamps on and off. In his senior year, Brush developed an electric light using a lamp and battery, all of his own construction.

Brush earned a degree in mining engineering from the University of Michigan (no electrical engineering programs existed at the time). Decades later, a classmate remembered, "We looked down upon him; we would scarcely acknowledge that he was one of us. He took the scientific course and we were in the literary department. The literary fellows were the dictators of college life and set themselves up on a self-supposed eminence that dwarfed all other departments." The classmate continued, "Ask any of us today of our class and the answer is certain to be 'I belong to the class of '69—Brush's class.'"

Returning to Cleveland from college, Brush worked in a combination residence and laboratory on Prospect Avenue. One of his experiments to perfect a commercially viable arc light resulted in an explosion that rocked the building. The landlord forced Brush to remove the laboratory, which the promising young inventor soon relocated to a building on Public Square.

When Brush built his first dynamo (electric generator), he transported it to his father's farm in Euclid Township. There he tested his creation using two horses to supply the initial power. Brush entered an improved version in a highly competitive contract bid for the Franklin Institute. Following months of intense testing, the institute selected the Brush generator, ranking it far superior to competitors. Winning the contract provided Brush with the publicity and prestige to profitably market generators for industrial uses.

On April 29, 1879, Brush entered the public street lighting market with a dramatic demonstration of his arc lights on Cleveland's Public Square. The thrilling event marked the first use of electricity to illuminate a city street.

Two years earlier, Brush had attempted to brighten downtown Cleveland by fastening a prototype of his arc light to a window in his Public Square laboratory. Deciding to add an extra attraction to a parade already in progress, Brush activated his new invention as the procession marched past the lab. Befuddled horses in the pageant nearly panicked as they reared and pranced in confused bewilderment. A police officer entered Brush's business, ordering him to turn out the distracting light. The episode ended Brush's first attempt at illuminating the heart of downtown Cleveland.

But the spring evening in 1879 belonged to Brush. The primary demonstration involved lighting twelve lamps, each one fastened to its own 150-foot ornamental pole and emitting the equivalent of two thousand candlepower. The first lamp flickered on about 8:00 p.m.; the other eleven followed in rapid order to create a dramatic purplish hue over Public Square. A few onlookers expressed disappointment, expecting the lights to totally mimic daylight. But the vast majority of observers marveled at this now radiant sector of downtown Cleveland.

With the lighting of the twelfth lamp, cannons boomed from the lakeshore to signal the beginning of a colossal celebration. The Cleveland Grays military band provided the music. Singers, paying homage to the marvelous occasion, performed the specially composed song "The New Electric Light":

While strolling thru the park one eve
I saw some funny sights
That appeared to me beneath the glare
Of the new electric lights.

A nice young couple passed me
And I heard a sly request,
Will you take me for your husband?
And I heard her answer, "Yes."

Right: A young Charles Brush entered the business world by developing the first commercially successful arc light. *Courtesy of the* Plain Dealer.

Below: Charles Brush's manufacturing facility, located at Hough Avenue and Forty-third Street, closed in 1896 after he exited from the electrical industry. *Courtesy of Cleveland Public Library, Photograph Collection.*

The new electric light—
On any pleasant night;
You'll see some funny pictures
By the new electric light.

Cleveland's political leaders immediately contracted with Brush to brighten Public Square for one year. He charged one dollar per hour to use his twelve already-installed arc lights. Cities throughout the world soon teamed with Brush to provide street lighting. His fast-growing Brush Electric Company successfully fulfilled lucrative agreements in New York, Boston, Tokyo, Shanghai, San Francisco, Philadelphia, Baltimore, Montreal and cities in India and Australia. A three-quarter-mile stretch of Broadway Avenue in New York, illuminated by twenty-three Brush arc lights, became known as "The Great White Way." Brush also invented a low-cost carbon to operate the arc lamps, and Cleveland soon led the world in the manufacture of commercial carbons.

The usage of Brush electric arc lights quickly spread to other applications. *Scientific American* reported in 1881 that the lights had been successfully implemented in factories, stores, hotels, churches, parks, docks, railroad depots, mines and John Wanamaker's famous Philadelphia department store. At the age of thirty-one, Brush reigned as the most successful pioneer in the field of commercial illumination.

Yet few people today, even among Clevelanders, recognize Brush as a groundbreaker in inventing practical electrical applications. As the 1880s unfolded, Brush witnessed intense cutthroat competition, vicious corporate personality clashes, overbearing politicians and stern scrutiny from Wall Street investors. Rather than participating in one of the Gilded Age's fiercest and most bizarre illustrations of business rivalry, Brush instead sold his company, never to reenter the electric industry.

In 1887, with money pouring in from his company's earnings, the once-poor farm boy constructed one of Euclid Avenue's most lavish homes. The nearly forty-thousand-square-foot mansion, attesting to his business aplomb and affluence, required more than two years to construct. Louis Tiffany's company designed stained-glass windows, lighting fixtures and skylights; oak from England and rosewood from Japan beautified the home. Wall paintings, acquired throughout the world, exceeded $1 million in value. When he entertained guests, Brush added a personal touch by playing a massive pipe organ whose first-floor console pipes extended to the mansion's third-floor ballroom. Guests enjoyed billiard

Built in 1887, Charles Brush's mansion graced Euclid Avenue for a mere forty-three years. *Courtesy of Cleveland Public Library, Photograph Collection.*

Charles Brush's backyard windmill generated the first electricity used in a Cleveland home. *Courtesy of Special Collections, Michael Schwartz Library, Cleveland State University.*

matches with Brush, a very accomplished player. A private basement laboratory allowed Brush to conduct research and experimentation in many different disciplines.

To his neighbors' amazement (and mostly chagrin), Brush designed and built an eighty-thousand-pound backyard windmill, fifty-six feet in diameter and sixty feet tall. The remarkable contraption charged ten tons of storage batteries, more than enough energy to electrify his home.

Millionaires race down Euclid Avenue past the Brush (left) and still existing Beckwith mansions. *Courtesy of Special Collections, Michael Schwartz Library, Cleveland State University.*

Meanwhile, Brush's success with arc lighting fostered formidable competition. Thomas Edison correctly envisioned a vast market for indoor home lighting and perfected the incandescent light bulb to capture that market. In New York, while Brush lit up Broadway, Edison crews dug trenches to bury the wires needed to bring electricity into the city's homes.

By 1885, more than six hundred lighting companies operated throughout the world. Gas companies fought a valiant but futile battle to defeat electricity's encroachments into their territories. In the meantime, William Sawyer, an Edison competitor, shot and killed a man following an argument regarding the merits of Edison's light bulb.

In the 1880s, Brush witnessed arguably the hardest-fought and weirdest illustrations of nineteenth-century corporate conflict. Alleged copyright infringements fostered hundreds, if not thousands, of simultaneous patent lawsuits. The infamous "current war" pitted Edison's use of direct current (DC) against the alternating current (AC) endorsed by George Westinghouse. When compared with DC, AC technology transmitted electricity over substantially larger distances at a lower cost, but the transmission required a higher voltage level. Nikola Tesla's polyphase system improved the performance of alternating current.

Facing this hard-hitting competition, Edison stressed safety issues, real or fabricated, associated with the transmission of high-voltage alternating current. Direct current advocates blamed alternating current for several electrocution deaths caused by live wires. In fact, the DC enthusiasts even called for an outright legal ban on the use of alternating current.

To vividly demonstrate the dangers of alternating current, the Edison camp staged horrifying electrocutions of dogs in the presence of scientists, public health officials, politicians, newspaper reporters and physicians. The suffering canines generally required only about three hundred volts of alternating current to send them to their agonizing deaths, while comparable killing with direct current required nearly one thousand volts. To better mimic the size of humans, DC supporters extended the slaughter to horses.

As the war between competing currents continued, its scope expanded from annihilating animals to killing humans. Dialogue concerning the use of the Brush generator to inflict capital punishment began as early as 1880. Later in the decade, Harold P. Brown (a previously obscure engineer now secretly paid by Edison) purchased a used Westinghouse generator and commandeered other Westinghouse equipment to construct the world's first electric chair, in the process once again publicizing the perceived danger of alternating current. On August 6, 1890, William Kemmler, who had used an axe to kill a woman posing as his wife, entered history as the first criminal to be electrocuted. Kemmler received one thousand volts of alternating current for seventeen seconds but remained alive although in agonizing pain. A second one-thousand-volt dosage, this one administered for sixty seconds, finally killed the criminal. Adding a new verb to the vernacular, proponents of direct current called criminal electrocutions "Westinghousing" and those electrocuted as being "Westinghoused."

As the corporate war continued, Brown challenged Westinghouse to an electrical duel; the two scientists would simultaneously be subjected to an equal amount of voltage, Brown with direct current and Westinghouse with alternating. Current would be inflicted into their bodies at increasing increments of fifty volts. The contest would continue until one of the foes either conceded defeat or died. Westinghouse declined to participate in the competition.

At the Chicago (Columbian) World's Fair, General Electric displayed a giant eight-foot, half-ton incandescent light bulb that generated pulsating light that changed its color and shape. But a huge bulb proved rather inadequate when compared with the Westinghouse exhibit, where Nikola Tesla lighted up himself. Passing between 250,000 and one million volts of electricity through his body, Tesla generated dazzling beams of illumination, even lighting lamps using his own body as an electrical conductor. Wearing unusually thick-soled shoes, standing on a wooden footstool, using props consisting of heavy steel cylinders mounted on steel pedestals (all placed on wooden bases) and most likely other devices, Tesla survived by not creating a ground voltage between his body and the electrical generator.

By 1889, Brush had witnessed enough of the electric industry's discord. Although possessing good business senses, he appeared more interested in creating inventions rather than corporate empires. He and major stockholders sold controlling interest in the Brush business to the Thomson-Houston Company, soon to be an important part of General Electric. That same year, the new Edison General Electric Company consolidated several smaller Edison companies, located in different states, into one integrated business.

Development of large-scale power distribution systems and the mass production of consumer and industrial products required vast investments of money. Edison and Westinghouse turned to Wall Street to acquire the enormous amounts of capital needed to continue their aggressive company expansions; neither escaped personal misfortune in the process. The scientists, even though capable businessmen, could not match the bloodthirsty approach to making a profit exhibited by the investment community.

The money brokers merged Edison's company with Thomson-Houston to form General Electric, never informing Edison in advance of their actions nor advising him that the new company would no longer bear his name. General Electric pushed Edison aside and immediately invested in AC transmission. Westinghouse also lost control of his company to financial interests. Tesla died in poverty. Early in 1891, Brush completely severed ties with the company still bearing his name. Integrated into General Electric, the Brush Electric Company lost its separate identity.

Brush continued to pursue scientific and intellectual interests for the remainder of his long life but none directly related to electricity. Into his seventies, he still walked most days more than thirty blocks down Euclid Avenue from his mansion to his office in the downtown Arcade, the landmark office building he helped finance. Brush spent his final birthday in his laboratory developing a kinetic theory of gravitation. At the time, he doubted the complete accuracy of Einstein's theory of relativity and searched to discover faults and inconsistencies in Einstein's work.

Rather than subjecting his residence to probable urban decay, Brush specified the mansion must be torn down upon his death. The forced

A private basement laboratory allowed Brush to conduct research and experimentation in many different disciplines, including his creative mechanical explanations of gravity. *Courtesy of Special Collections, Michael Schwartz Library, Cleveland State University.*

destruction paved the way for one of Cleveland's most memorable venues, the Cleveland Arena. In 1990, the Cleveland chapter of the American Red Cross constructed its new headquarters that encompassed much of the land where the Brush mansion and Cleveland Arena once stood.

Chapter 16

The Demise of Guardian Trust

H enry Payne McIntosh served as either president or chairman of the board of the Guardian Savings and Trust Company for thirty-five of the company's thirty-nine-year existence. Sadly, before his 1935 death from heart failure at the age of eighty-nine, McIntosh witnessed the bank's total collapse and a prison sentence for the handpicked heir who had assumed his position as president.

Born in Cleveland in 1846 to poor Scottish immigrants, McIntosh supported himself as a teen by working as a telegraph operator for the Cleveland and Erie Railroad. Following a twelve-year stint working in Alliance, he returned to Cleveland. In

Henry Payne McIntosh began his career as a telegraph operator and eventually became a distinguished banker with a national reputation. *Courtesy of Cleveland Public Library, Photograph Collection.*

In 1914, Guardian Trust acquired the former New England Building on Euclid Avenue. National City Bank later used the building. *Courtesy of Cleveland Public Library, Photograph Collection.*

1885, as an employee of the Citizens Telegraph & Telephone Company, McIntosh amazed the city's executives with a demonstration of long-distance telephone calling, the world's latest technological invention. To most everyone's amazement, a Cleveland contingent conducted a clear conversation with a similar group of businessmen in New York City.

In the 1890s, Mark Hanna and others successfully lobbied for laws making the establishment of trust companies easier; these laws led to the creation of both the Guardian Trust and Cleveland Trust banks. On December 10, 1894, Guardian Savings and Trust opened its doors in the Wade Building at the intersection of West Ninth Street and Superior Avenue. Invited civic dignitaries and newspapermen inspected the company's plush new offices and enjoyed an elegant lunch, followed by the smoking of expensive cigars.

Four years after Guardian's debut, McIntosh assumed the presidency of the company, an organization then possessing about $1,500,000 in assets. Within twenty years, Guardian boasted the largest office building in Cleveland (the still-existing New England Building on Euclid Avenue). In 1917, when McIntosh retired as president to assume leadership as chairman of the board, Guardian Trust's deposits had accumulated to about $52 million. During his years as bank president, he joined the city's social elite by acquiring a Millionaires' Row home and a summer retreat in Wickliffe-on-the-Lake. In addition to his splendid banking career, McIntosh served as president or director of several railroads.

Thirteen years after its construction in 1894, Henry P. McIntosh purchased this twenty-four-room stone mansion on Euclid Avenue near East Seventy-first Street. *Courtesy of Special Collections, Michael Schwartz Library, Cleveland State University.*

Executives of Guardian Savings required little debate in selecting J. Arthur House as McIntosh's presidential successor. Born in Cleveland in 1871, House withdrew from Central High School without completing his education. His employment at Guardian Trust began in 1894 as one of the bank's four original employees. In twenty-three years, his upward progression included positions as clerk, teller, assistant cashier, assistant secretary, secretary, fifth vice-president, first vice-president and finally president. He worked closely with McIntosh, his friend and mentor. In fact, the two even shared the same office. At the onset of the Depression, the bank had established twenty-six subsidiaries doing business in investments and real estate. House, Cleveland's highest-salaried bank president, earned $90,000 annually with another $15,000 in bonuses.

Recognized as an astute banker, House served as one of twelve members of the Federal Advisory Council. This select committee, composed of one member from each Federal Reserve district, provided the Federal Reserve in Washington with advice and assistance during the difficult first years of the Depression. Acquiring a national reputation, House acted as toastmaster at an annual dinner of United States trust company executives held at the Waldorf-Astoria Hotel in New York.

In 1933, with McIntosh as chairman of the board and House as president, the Guardian Trust Company failed. On February 25, the bank lost half of its deposits on that single day. The next week, following Franklin Roosevelt's National Bank Holiday, Guardian Trust never reopened. Depositors initially received one cent on a dollar along with another twenty cents in 1934.

House voluntarily resigned to allow a smooth restructuring of the bank (which never occurred). In a subsequent investigation, auditors discovered numerous illegal dealings and, hidden from the company's books, a series of loans, bonuses and Christmas presents to bank officers and directors. When the bank collapsed, unpaid loans to the bank's management totaled $3,927,785.49, including $235,778.00 owed by House. McIntosh and his son accounted for another $137,913.35.

In an improper attempt to improve the company's reported financial condition, executives reported more than $7 million in outstanding checks as deposits. Auditors also uncovered never-recorded transactions in which money had been borrowed from the company's pension and retirement fund to purchase Guardian Trust stock. A federal court jury, composed of seven women and five men, debated for three hours and fifteen minutes before finding House guilty of twenty-six counts of misapplication of funds and

INTEREST

totaling

$28,681,400

has been paid to Guardian savings depositors

since 1894. How much of that has been YOURS?

You CAN begin to share NOW. Savings deposited

January 3, 4 or 5 earn interest from January 1.

GUARDIAN
TRUST COMPANY

By 1933, Guardian Savings had paid more than $28 million in interest. But the financial institution would never pay its depositors another penny. *Courtesy of the* Plain Dealer.

ten counts of false entries. Sentenced to six years in federal prison, House appealed the verdict to the Unites States Circuit Court of Appeals and then to the Supreme Court, but both courts reaffirmed the jury's decision. House received a parole after serving two years of the term.

In 1935, at the age of eighty-nine, McIntosh died of a heart attack near Jacksonville while traveling on a train bound for Cleveland. Eight years later, the once-wealthy House declared bankruptcy, claiming $2,118,394 in liabilities and $468 in assets. On February 19, 1952, after years of legal maneuverings, the court finally dissolved Guardian Trust.

Beginning in 1929, McIntosh's Euclid Avenue home functioned as an apartment. From 1947 into 1965, Ace Motor Sales operated a used car lot on the property, although the home remained standing. In 1966, a newspaper advertisement invited interested parties to come to the old home to find out how to "get rich quick in the home improvement field." Today, the Masjid Bilal Mosque encompasses the McIntosh site and additional eastern land.

Bibliography

Brady, Kathleen. *Ida Tarbell: Portrait of a Muckraker*. Pittsburgh, PA: University of Pittsburgh Press, 1989.

Cigliano, Jan. *Showplace of America: Cleveland's Euclid Avenue, 1850–1910*. Kent, OH: Kent State University Press, 1991.

Condon, George E. *Cleveland: Prodigy of the Western Reserve*. Tulsa, OK: Continental Heritage Press, 1979.

————. *Cleveland: The Best Kept Secret*. New York: Doubleday & Company, 1967.

Crosbie, John S. *The Incredible Mrs. Chadwick*. New York: McGraw-Hill, 1975.

Freeberg, Ernest. *The Age of Edison*. New York: Penguin Press, 2013.

Goulder, Grace. *John D. Rockefeller: The Cleveland Years*. Cleveland, OH: Western Reserve Historical Society, 1972.

Hamen, Susan E. *John D. Rockefeller: Entrepreneur & Philanthropist*. Edina, MN: ABDO Publishing Company, 2011.

Hanna, Marcus Alonzo. *His Book*. Boston: Chapple Publishing Company, 1904.

Johnson, Tom L. *My Story*. New York: B.W. Huebsch, 1911.

Jonnes, Jill. *Empires of Light: Edison, Tesla, Westinghouse, and the Race to Electrify the World*. New York: Random House Trade Paperbacks, 2004.

Klein, Maury. *The Power Makers: Steam, Electricity, and the Men Who Invented Modern America*. New York: Bloomsbury Press, 2008.

Losser, Carol. "A Tale of Two Josephines: Class, Gender and Self-Sovereignty in the Gilded Age." *Gender & History* 13, no. 1 (April 2001): 65–96.

Rose, William Ganson. *Cleveland: The Making of a City*. Kent, OH: Kent State University Press, 1990.

Schwarz, Ted. *Cleveland Curiosities*. Charleston, SC: The History Press, 2010.

Tarbell, Ida M. *History of the Standard Oil Company*. 2 vols. New York: Peter Smith, 1950.

Weinbert, Steve. *Taking On the Trust: The Epic Battle of Ida Tarbell and John D. Rockefeller*. New York: W.W. Norton & Company, 2008.

Wilson, Ella Grant. *Famous Old Euclid Avenue of Cleveland*. Cleveland, OH: Evangelican Press, 1932.

———. *Famous Old Euclid Avenue of Cleveland*. Vol. 2. Cleveland, OH: Wilson, 1937.

Index

About the Author

Native Clevelander Alan Dutka is a retired executive. During his business career, he authored four marketing research books, including *Customer Satisfaction Research*, a primary selection of the Newbridge Executive Book Club that has been translated into Spanish and Japanese editions. Since his retirement, he has published five other Cleveland history books: *AsiaTown Cleveland: From Tong Wars to Dim Sum*; *Cleveland Calamities: A History of Storm, Fire and Pestilence*; *East Fourth Street: The Rise, Decline, and Rebirth of an Urban Cleveland Street*; *Cleveland's Short Vincent: The Theatrical Grill and Its Notorious Neighbors*; and *Cleveland in the Gilded Age: A Stroll down Millionaires' Row* (coauthored with Dan Ruminski). Dutka is a popular speaker at historical societies, libraries and community centers.

Printed in the USA
CPSIA information can be obtained
at www.ICGtesting.com
CBHW051932301024
16653CB00035B/8